PRAISE FOR DEATH ON HOLD

"Burt and Anita Folsom capture an amazing story of hope in *Death on Hold*. The story of Mitch, an Alabama man described as worthless by *Time* magazine, demonstrates his real worth in God. A great read for Christians and non-Christians alike."

—CRAIG DEROCHE, EXECUTIVE DIRECTOR, JUSTICE FELLOWSHIP

"Death on Hold is a modern-day book of Acts and shines a light on one of the most promising mission fields in America today: her bulging prisons."

—DAVID DURELL, TRUSTEE, MISSIONCOLUMBUS

"A real-life example of how faith can allow a person to 'create' purpose and meaning in life rather than passively waiting to find it."

—DR. KENT HAWKINS, HEAD OF PASTORAL CARE AND
COUNSELING, MOUNT PARAN CHURCH, ATLANTA, GEORGIA

"Anita and Burt Folsom tell a captivating and inspirational story of God's redemptive power, reminding us that we are called to love all of God's children, including those who are hardest to forgive. When we do so, we encounter God's redemptive power in our own lives, just as Mitchell Rutledge did."

—CHERYL BACHELDER, CEO, POPEYES
LOUISIANA KITCHEN, INC.

"In Mitch's story, told in his own voice, the poverty, loneliness, confusion and hopelessness of a stolen childhood come through with visceral impact. When, in the providence of God, unlikely individuals respond with love and hope, they become conduits of His Grace. After reading this book, the words of Jesus in Matthew 25:36, 'I was in prison, and ye came unto me,' will take on a renewed significance."

—DAVID KENT, SENIOR PASTOR, FELLOWSHIP
OF PRAISE CHURCH, STAFFORD, TEXAS

"*Death on Hold* is a powerful and engaging narrative. It has the power to change lives. I hope that jail and prison ministries around the world will use this book to help inmates live more successful lives, whether in jail or on the outside. Mitchell Rutledge's story is a warning about the tremendous damage that drugs can bring into anyone's life. But there is redemption and a new beginning, once he turns from his old ways and begins to build a better life."

— CAROL SWAIN, PROFESSOR OF LAW AND
  POLITICAL SCIENCE, VANDERBILT UNIVERSITY;
  AUTHOR; AND TELEVISION HOST

"I started reading *Death On Hold* and could not put it down. What a powerful story! I've worked with inner-city ministry in Houston for more than twenty years, and Mitchell Rutledge's story is a special triumph of God's grace over death and despair."

— PRINCE COUISNARD, PRESIDENT,
  MALACHI DESTINY AND PURPOSE

"Mitch's story is truly remarkable and a beautiful reminder of the inherent dignity that everyone has, which can only come from our creator. It is also a vivid reminder of how reconnecting with Christ, no matter what our past, is the only way to redemption. Burton and Anita Folsom have demonstrated what it looks like to live out the gospel, making this is a must-read and a reminder that, in Christ, not one of us is forgotten nor should we be discarded."

— DR. ANNE BRADLEY, VICE PRESIDENT FOR
  ECONOMIC INITIATIVES AT THE INSTITUTE
  FOR FAITH, WORK, AND ECONOMICS

DEATH ON HOLD

DEATH ON HOLD

A PRISONER'S DESPERATE PRAYER AND THE UNLIKELY
FAMILY WHO BECAME GOD'S ANSWER

BURTON FOLSOM AND ANITA FOLSOM

NELSON
BOOKS

An Imprint of Thomas Nelson

Published in Nashville, Tennessee, by Nelson Books, an imprint of Thomas Nelson. Nelson Books and Thomas Nelson are registered trademarks of HarperCollins Christian Publishing, Inc.

Thomas Nelson titles may be purchased in bulk for educational, business, fund-raising, or sales promotional use. For information, please e-mail SpecialMarkets@ThomasNelson.com.

Scripture quotations are taken from the Holy Bible, New International Version®, NIV®. Copyright © 1973, 1978, 1984, 2011 by Biblica, Inc.™ Used by permission of Zondervan. All rights reserved worldwide. www.zondervan.com

Some names have been changed.

Library of Congress Cataloging-in-Publication Data

Folsom, Burton W.
   Death on hold : a prisoner's desperate prayer and the unlikely family who became God's answer / Burton and Anita Folsom.
      pages cm
   Includes bibliographical references.
   ISBN 978-1-59555-600-4
   1. Rutledge, Mitchell, 1959- 2. Death row inmates--Alabama--Biography.
   3. Criminals--Rehabilitation--Alabama. 4. Prisoners--Religious life--Alabama.
   I. Folsom, Anita. II. Title.
   HV9468.R88F65 2015
   364.66092--dc23
   [B]   2014033243

Printed in the United States of America

15 16 17 18 19 RRD 6 5 4 3 2 1

*This book is dedicated to the men and women
currently on death row. May they find
encouragement, hope, and peace as they read it.*

CONTENTS

CONTENTS

CONTENTS

AUTHORS' NOTE

This is the story of the redemption of Mitchell Rutledge. It is not an analysis of his crime, nor is it a study of why some people fall through the cracks in society and don't get the help they need.

First, it is the story of an illiterate boy trying to find his way in a world of drugs, prostitution, and poverty. As a young man, Mitch finally hits bottom. In the midst of the biggest crisis of his life, alone and friendless, he reaches out and learns that miracles do happen.

We became friends with Mitchell Rutledge more than thirty years ago. Slowly at first, and then more regularly, Mitch told us the details of his life. In 2009, Burt asked Mitch to write down his life story, beginning with his earliest memories. In prison, Mitch could only send out mail with four pages per letter, so the episodes of his life became handwritten letters on notebook paper, four pages at a time. Because many of these memories were disjointed, we often went back to Mitch with questions; at times we looked up more background information on events he witnessed firsthand, such as the executions at Holman Prison. We interviewed Mitch's lawyer and other new "family members" who have become a part of Mitch's life. Then we supplemented Mitch's letters with poems he had written, beginning on death row and continuing for many years.

As part of a small group—Mitch's new "family"—we wanted to write his story as a warning to young people who are dabbling in drugs. We wanted to write his story as a hymn of rejoicing over what the Lord has done. And we wanted to write his story to draw attention to the fact that Mitch has been in prison since 1981. Having the story told by Mitch, as he lived it, seems to be the most powerful way to engage our readers in this amazing life.

Mitch wants to make a difference in society to keep young people from following his path to prison. At the same time, overcrowding in prisons is forcing states to release thousands of inmates. Mitch's record of time served and good behavior should make him a candidate for parole. At this point, Mitch can do more good outside of prison than being locked inside for the rest of his life.

That is why we wrote this book.

Burton and Anita Folsom

1

THIS IS MY STORY

Time magazine, "An Eye for an Eye," January 24, 1983:

> Death row is about the same size in Alabama [as in other states], where 55 men await the [electric] chair in Holman. Mitchell Rutledge, 23 years old, I.Q. 84, is among them. . . . To most people the life of a foolish punk like Rutledge does not count for much. He is defective. His death would not be unbearably sad. . . . There are guys not *worth* killing. Let Rutledge sit and stew in his 8-ft. by 5-ft. pen in Alabama. Forget him.[1]

Those are powerful words, and even today they startle me. Why? Because I am Mitchell Rutledge. *Time* was mostly right with its facts. I was illiterate—I could not read or write at all. I had no friends. I had no family that cared. My mother was dead and my father deserted me at birth. I was constantly in trouble as a teenager. I spent years in jail and prison, and then I killed a guy and was on death row waiting to die.

I told *Time* magazine, "I just want to let everybody know that I am sorry for what I did," and they said, "He is defective. Forget him."

Forget him? I was already forgotten. But I cried out to God for friends, and I cried out to God to give my life meaning and purpose. It was at that point that He put my death on hold. This is my story.

I was born in October 1959, but my mother was still a kid herself: only thirteen years old. I never knew my father. We lived in Columbus, Georgia, most of the time. Sometimes my mother took me to my grandmother's house, and sometimes I lived in an apartment with my mother.

When my mother was about sixteen, she was sent to reform school, so then I lived with my grandmother. Once my mother was released, we were back together. I can remember staying with this aunt or that aunt every weekend because my mother would be out doing other things. My mother would pack me a few clothes and off we would go to one of my mother's aunts for the weekend. I liked it because it meant eating candy or maybe getting a quarter to spend.

Fridays were very big days for my cousin Perry and me. I can remember homemade ice cream made by Great Aunt Dewbell. She had a cat, and I'm afraid of cats. I still remember sitting on top of something to get away from that cat as I was eating her homemade ice cream.

I usually wouldn't see my mother for two or three days. This was every week. I called her "Little Mommy." She wasn't but seventeen when I was four. After the weekend, she would come to get me and we would go home.

BLACK AND WHITE

A poem written years later by Mitchell Rutledge

> *Christmas was coming.*
> *I knew I couldn't get that much.*
> *Asked for a cowboy suit*
> *A black one.*
> *Yes, the bad guy.*
> *Played with my cousin*
> *He wore white.*
> *Yes, the good guy.*
> *I shot him.*
> *Cap pistol.*
> *Hit him too.*
> *Got a beating for it.*

When I was a young teenager, I had a choice: I could stay in school or I could operate in the streets. I chose to be on the streets most of the time because that's where I had confidence and a chance to excel. School wasn't much of an option because I couldn't read. That meant I couldn't succeed academically.

I don't want to be too hard on the public schools because I was a tough case for them. But no teacher ever helped me learn to read when I was in the early grades; they just passed me through social promotion. By the time I was enrolled in Baker High School in Columbus, Georgia, I was told to bring a pen and paper to a special class for students not doing well with their studies. We were all from broken homes, and none of us had any money. I wasn't sure I could learn anything out of a book. Were we incapable of learning? That was the message the school was sending us, and no teaching took place. We did nothing and stayed until lunch—it was a way to get a meal that day—and then most of us left for the streets.

As I said, my mother gave birth to me at age thirteen. She then had three more children—Anton, Jackson, and the youngest, Caroline—with three different fathers. Caroline's father was in the military and was transferred to Germany. He offered to marry my mother and take her, Caroline, Anton, and Jackson with him to Germany. But not me. My mother—to her credit—wouldn't leave me behind alone. She ended up deciding not to go, but after he left she did need the allotment check he sent us each month. His payments became irregular, and then they completely stopped.

I was fourteen, almost fifteen, when the payments stopped. After a while a German lady sent a letter to my mother, and I found out why the cash had stopped coming. Her letter said that he (Caroline's father) loved her and no longer loved my mother. In fact, they were planning to get married and did so and had a child. As my mother read the letter, she was crying more and more with each sentence, even each word. As my mother bawled and bawled, I found myself hating him more and more.

I also felt more drawn to my mother because, after all, she hadn't gone with him to Germany because she didn't want to desert me. Now she was deserted. After a month or so, my mother had to go to the hospital for about a week. My two brothers and my sister went to live with my mother's family in Phenix City, Alabama. I went along, too, because she wanted me there and I was in an obliging mood. But I was still planning to be a part of our hood in nearby Columbus because that's where my friends were.

I would check in with my grandmother from time to time to let her know I wasn't dead. When my mother got out of the hospital, we all went back to Columbus, Georgia. But disaster had struck. Our home had been broken into. We didn't have much, but what we did have was now gone. My mother's prized possession was a very small color TV, and now that was gone.

That next year, at fifteen, I began selling drugs—or I should say, fake drugs. I picked that up by listening and watching. And I almost didn't make it to age sixteen.

One night at about two in the morning, I was calling it a night and went to an area of downtown Columbus that was full of black-owned clubs and businesses. Drugs, prostitutes, and pimps were all over the area. I was walking by a place called Top Hat and stopped in to get some chicken.

I started again for home and a black guy, maybe about fifty years old, driving a red Thunderbird, stopped and asked me if I wanted a ride. I had seen that car in the area before, so I said, "Okay." Once I got in, he asked where I lived. I said, "Georgia Terrace Apartments."

Then he asked, "Do you have to go home right now?"

Hearing that question raised my antenna at once, so I said, "Yes, I have to go right away."

Then I saw him reach down on the side of his seat, next to the dash on the driver's side, and he was coming up with a gun. I immediately jumped out of the car, which was not easy because we were going at least twenty-five miles an hour. I hit the ground. He stopped the car to come after me, and I yelled at the top of my lungs, "Help, help! He's trying to kill me!"

We had reached a residential area, so some lights came on and fortunately for me, he drove off. God was with me right then. I was in a lot of pain, but I made it home. My mom was upset with my appearance and my lateness and was even more upset when I explained to her what had happened. I had made some money selling drugs that night, however, so at least we could have food the next day.

FOOD

by Mitchell Rutledge, written years after his childhood

It goes without saying,
I came up very poor.
Which means there were times when there
      wasn't anything.
At an early age I can't remember
The importance of food.
Food had no real value to it
Because I looked at it the same way
I looked at everything else given to me
At that time on a regular basis.
How was that?
The same way I looked at night and day.
It came and went
Without any knowledge of where it come from.
But once I became older
Old enough to understand the importance of it
Everything became clear.
Now it was different for me.
I was aware
There was no food to eat
In the house for the moment.
There was more to it
Than just eating it or desiring it.
All types of questions were coming into play.
At the sight of no food

My heart went out to my younger brothers,
Sister and mom.
Not myself, why?
Because I was 15
I could take care of myself.
So I decided to bring
Some of the stolen things to the house.
If there was money I would give that.
At that age I was also very selfish and into
    image.
Yes, the look.
That cost money, if you can't steal it.
I really didn't like being around the house
With all those things going on.
No food, no money, it was very sad.
I consider this to be the lowest moment in
    my life.
My mother is in her room,
My two brothers and one sister in the living
    room.
I walk into the house,
Walk into the kitchen,
Open the refrigerator,
I find one jug of water . . .
The only thing in the refrigerator.
My heart fell to my feet.
I walked into my mother's room
And asked her, "Have you and the kids ate?"

She started to cry.
I went and got something for them to eat.
I hadn't been home for days.
It was a major turnaround in my life.

2

TRAGEDY

The year after the break-in at our apartment, I was out one day spending time with my friend Jerry. My mother called Jerry's mother and then spoke with me, asking me to come home because I had been gone for three days. So I went home. When I opened the door, my mother said, "Boy, where you been?" Before I could respond, she said, "Get in there and get you something to eat." So I did. While I was eating, she called me. I answered and she said, "Come here."

I thought I was about to get reprimanded for being gone so long, so I stayed in the kitchen to eat a little more before facing her. Then I opened the door to her bedroom and saw my mother with her head hanging over her shoulder as she lay on her back. I ran to her. I said, "Momma, Momma," as I shook her. After I saw there was no response, I flipped out. I called my aunt (her sister), and she called the ambulance. They arrived in about fifteen minutes, took my mother's pulse, and told me she was dead.

I felt terrible because I hadn't called the ambulance sooner and hadn't obeyed her instructions. I blamed myself. That whole situation stunned me. My mother was dead at age twenty-nine. The coroner wrote "pulmonary embolism" on the death certificate. My mother was gone.

Now, at age sixteen, I was really on my own. My brother Anton was farmed out to my grandmother's brother, and Jackson went to my grandmother's sister. My sister Caroline did best. She went to be with sweet Aunt Dewbell, my grandfather's aunt.

I went with my grandmother for about three months, and then I moved into an apartment. It had only one furnished room, which included a small kitchen. I shared a bathroom with other tenants. My grandmother gave me a stereo and a TV, so that was nice, but I had to pay $20 per week for rent, and that was not so nice. I had no job and wasn't able to get one. When I would go into a place looking for a job, they would give me a form. But since I couldn't read, I could never fill it out. I was ashamed to admit I couldn't read, and the employer wouldn't have hired me knowing I couldn't read. So between my pride and my lack of skills, I had no job.

What did I do? I lived off the streets. I robbed and I

stole. I dealt in prostitution, and my little apartment became a way station for runaway girls, many of whom ended up in prostitution. I didn't know how to cook and had no income. I just stole and lived mostly on the streets. That was my life for the next three years.

3

COLUMBUS, GEORGIA

The red-light district of Columbus, Georgia (population 150,000 in 1970),[1] was totally alive at night—especially through the eyes of a fifteen-year-old soon to be sixteen. My drug business worked this way: I started out selling "dummy drugs" to soldiers and young white guys who had come to the red-light district looking for action. Columbus was, and is, a soldier town because Fort Benning is about twelve miles away. The red-light district, and even beyond, had strip clubs all over.

"Dummy drugs" is just a street name for fake drugs. I went to the herb shop and bought some herb grass that looked just like real pot. Then I mixed the seeds from real pot in, so the mixture looked and smelled like real pot. I would buy a grocery bag of herb grass for one dollar and fix it all up to sell as marijuana. I also concocted some fake cocaine by using baking soda. Once I had packaged my stuff, I would go downtown.

I lived seven blocks from the red-light district. I discovered that soldiers and white college kids were the best sources for sales. Why? Because you could catch the college students and soldiers right there in the strip clubs drinking and looking for something to get high with. And they weren't too picky about what to use, especially after they'd had a couple of drinks. Almost all the women who ran the strip clubs were from Vietnam. Only the strippers were black or white.

I would go into the strip clubs and buy myself a beer— even though I was only fifteen or sixteen years old. I looked old enough to belong there—especially with my fake ID card, which said I was eighteen. Anyway, I would be there at a table with my beer, and I would begin to go from table to table letting the soldiers and students know I was the man with the drugs. After I returned to my table, it wouldn't be long before guys would come to me wanting to go in the bathroom to transact business.

To beat the competition, I always made my packages much bigger than the standard sizes—I was giving them a bargain. Once we began to dicker on price, I had to be fast and shrewd. After all, my stuff wasn't real. With the cocaine, I would use real cocaine for the taste test and then switch to baking soda when it was time to sell. Business went best when my clients were half drunk and not particular about taste tests. Still, I had to be alert and quick in doing business, because undercover cops were always around, looking for guys buying and selling drugs. The college kids especially didn't want to be hassled by the cops.

I had to be cautious because over time club owners began to sense who the drug dealers were. I did business in a club on First Avenue called the Burning Inferno. It was a top-of-the-line strip club for Columbus. They had stage shows with curtain calls and everything. Anyway, the staff there put the owner on to me one night. This German lady, about age fifty, walked up to me and asked me to step outside. I asked why. She said that she was the owner and heard I was selling drugs in her club. So we stepped outside. It was about eleven thirty.

Once we got outside in the light, she took one look at me and said, "Hey, you aren't eighteen years old. Why are you in my club?" I insisted I was eighteen and showed her my ID card. About that time, an officer came by on one of those three-wheeled carts. She stopped him, and I was about to take off running when she said, "He isn't old enough to be in my club." She didn't say anything about drugs, so I stayed and showed the cop my ID card. The cop looked at me and my ID and said, "Get something more official before going into the clubs," and then he left.

I was about to walk away when the club owner said, "Why aren't you home where kids should be at this time of night?"

I said, "Because I'm not a kid."

Then she asked, "What are you doing with earrings in both of your ears, like a girl?"

I explained that it was part of my identity—young blacks were beginning to do that in the 1970s. We talked for about an hour, and she asked me to meet her after the club closed, which was 2:00 a.m., at Ken and Company, a bar on Front Street. I was very excited because she obviously had money.

We met and talked some more, and we did that every night for about a week. After that, she took me to an apartment. It was very late, and I had to lie down in the car because she didn't want anyone to see me with her. Once we got to the apartment, she told me to stay in the car until she had unlocked the door. Then she waved me in.

This went on frequently for about four months until I saw her one afternoon, walking downtown. I was with my friend Jerry, and I wanted him to know that I knew her; she was with a girl who appeared to be about fourteen years old. I spoke to her as we passed, and she acted like she had never seen me before. She ignored me and didn't even look my way. That really hurt my feelings.

My friend Jerry began to make fun of me and called me a liar. Later that night I went back to the club, and she said it was over with me. I was stupid, she said. I should not have spoken to her while she was with her daughter. That hurt because she had said she was going to help me get off the streets. She owned the club with her husband, who was black, so I had thought he would be more likely to help me, but I lost an opportunity and hit the streets even harder after that.

Next came the runaways.

4

RUNAWAYS

Around this time, 1976 to 1977, many runaways came to Columbus, Georgia, especially to the downtown area. There was a particular place on Broadway called Hippie Square. It was open twenty-four hours a day, and there were rooms with waterbeds in them and chairs and, of course, all sorts of items used to get high. Drugs were easy to find inside Hippie Square. Rumors were the guys that worked there sold drugs, and I know that was true. I enjoyed going in and out of there, where young people from all over the United States were meeting up.

Frankly, there were a lot of beautiful girls hanging around, and so I always made myself appear as a savvy businessman. After all, I knew the ins and outs of the streets of Columbus. I hoped to appear suave enough to impress and attract the ladies. The fact that I had my own apartment impressed the crowd at Hippie Square, because it could be hard in the streets.

Since I had my own apartment, in time one or two young women approached me with the idea of spending one night with me. They said they needed a real night of sleep without worrying about the creeps on the street. I agreed. One night, however, would turn into weeks. They would continue to prostitute themselves to buy food and help with a few bills around the house.

I would come home, and they would be in my living room watching TV and smoking pot. Sometimes they would have money for me on the living room table under the ashtray. What I had given them was a place of refuge without putting much pressure on them. Eventually they all moved on. Sometimes I would see them again at Hippie Square, sometimes not.

This continued with a number of runaways until I had to move out of my apartment to escape the police, who had stopped me for having a gun on school property. Sometimes I would drive back to high school and hang out with some of my homeboys from my hood. We call kids from the hood "homeboys," and together we would steal cars. Sometimes we found guns in the stolen cars. One of my homeboys gave me a gun, so I was armed.

One particular day my friend Bobby and I went to pick up Bobby's girlfriend from school. While we were there, some guys from another hood were talking trash about our hood. This was part of our neighborhood wars. One thing led to another, and I let them know I had a gun. After everyone saw the gun, the other guys began to run. They knew our names and told the police about my having a gun.

To get away from the police, I went to live with Fifi, my mother's first cousin. This introduced me to another level of the street life because all my family and friends were street hustlers in those days, and I began to hustle with them. I learned a lot from pimps and prostitutes in the neighborhood. I worked with one pimp who took me with him into empty apartments to steal the different appliances that came with the apartments, and even the carpet from the floor.

I had moved to a new level because now I was with adults who were making their money stealing from hard-working people. So street life had a new perspective for me. I saw new things. For example, I saw women on drugs totally confused and selling themselves for more drugs. I saw some of them beaten because they wanted to come in out of the cold and put on more clothes. I saw junkies who had burned up all their veins, lying dazed in rooms that reeked of vomit and pot. I witnessed the ugly side of street life. I was in the midst of it and trying to make my way in this new adult world. My cousins and other junkies were my partners in crime.

For example, while the prostitutes in our group went to work, I would be nearby trying to rob the men. I had to be careful. Hotel rooms would be rented out so my prostitute friends could take their johns there. We had it all planned out. The prostitute would tell the john to keep his money on him and not to leave his money in his car because guys were breaking into cars. The prostitute assured the john that her pimp would not let anyone rob him because that would be bad for business. So the john would keep his money in the hotel room, the prostitute would turn off the lights, and then she would secretly unlock the door when the room was dark.

In a few minutes, I would sneak in the room while the john was occupied. Later, after the john realized he had been robbed, several of us would run into the room and try to scare him away. By the way, if possible, one of us would shake down his car—not only to rob it or strip it down but also to take any gun that might be there. We didn't want him returning to the scene of the robbery with a gun in his hand and revenge in his heart.

5

DRUGS

Life was moving fast for me, drugs were everywhere, and it was dangerous. People sometimes just disappeared. Life was not fair for anyone in that world.

One night a young woman about three years older than me came to me saying that she wanted to run away. I knew her, as I did most of the girls. Her pimp, a guy named Hot Dog, had her and two more black girls. Rumor was that he was shooting up all the money in dope as well as being abusive. She was from Augusta, Georgia, and she wanted me to leave Columbus and go back to Augusta with her. I went to my cousin Mumu for advice, and she told me that I was only being used by this Augusta girl and that she just wanted me to go and buy her the bus tickets, and so on. Mumu said I was a way out for her and once we got to Augusta she would desert me. So I told the Augusta girl no. A few months later, she made her escape. Hot Dog had stabbed one of the other girls in the eye, and the undercover cops beat him up real bad. Most of the girls had some favor with the undercover cops.

One day these cops picked me up in a strip club where I was playing pool in the back with a hardened drug dealer. When the cops came in, the dealer dropped his drugs on the floor and kicked them under the table. During the shakedown that followed, the cops found the dope on the floor. They were reluctant to arrest the known gangster because they thought he was maybe too dangerous for them, so they settled for me instead. They asked me—all four of them, two blacks and two whites—to go with them. They took me to the car and put me in the backseat between a black cop and a white cop.

After everyone was in, I said, "What's going on here? That wasn't my dope—I have never seen it before, and it wasn't near me in the room."

One of them said, "Shut up!" but I continued to chatter. One elbowed me in the side, and another said, "Drive." Another one took out a big pocketknife and told the driver, "Let's take him to the river. Let's kill him and throw him in."

Oddly, I wasn't as afraid as I should have been. I acted like I was scared out of my mind, however, and I started screaming and begging them not to kill me. I was only seventeen years old.

"Please don't kill me!" I shouted, but they continued their drive toward the river. Finally, when we came to the river, they let me out and roughed me up. When they saw I wouldn't break, they took me to the police station, closed the doors, and began beating me some more. They wanted me to become an informer for them on all the illegal activity in my neighborhood.

During the beating, I formed a strategy. I said I was only fifteen years old and that I was going to report what they were doing to a minor to my mom and dad, who would then sue the police department. Suddenly, the white officer behind the desk opened a drawer that had all types of drugs in it. He pulled some out and said, "If you do that, we will say we found this on you."

They were making a deal with me, so I knew I would survive this run-in. If I kept my mouth shut, they would not press a drug charge on me.

As I was walking out the door, one of the black officers kicked me hard in my butt, and all of them began to laugh. After I made it back to my neighborhood, I explained to people in detail what had happened, and they laughed too. Maybe they thought it was funny, but I knew that I had held my own with the officers, and I had refused to be an informer for them.

6

JOB CORPS TO PRISON

Despite being arrested, I didn't repent and I continued
my street life. It was like a job. People hustled seven days a
week, and some made a good living. However, prison was
always right around the corner. Before I went to prison,
though, I was in the Job Corps in Morganfield, Kentucky.

As a teenager who had several run-ins with the police,
the local authorities in Columbus told me that they were
sending me to the Job Corps. I wasn't sure what that was, but
it sounded better than reform school or jail. My transporta-
tion was arranged by the staff in one of the city government
offices, and before I knew it, I was out of Georgia and on
my way to Kentucky. I was supposed to be trained as a
welder, but I never learned anything about welding. I did do

well in advanced fighting. In fact, after four months in Job Corps, I was kicked out for gang fighting.

At Job Corps, I had a new girlfriend named Billie from Selma, Alabama. I'm ashamed to say I don't even remember her last name. Being irresponsible, I got her pregnant. Shortly after she told me the news, I was kicked out of Job Corps and then she was also kicked out for getting pregnant. She insisted on having the baby, but she and I fought more and more with each other—over little things. We broke up and I split. To this day, I don't know if my child was a boy or girl. I think about my son or daughter many nights. I had reproduced and perpetuated my failure on another generation.

After my Job Corps debut, I went back to Alabama and soon ended up in prison. I was actually innocent of the crime that got me sent to prison the first time. Of course, I had committed many crimes that I got away with, so maybe my conviction was needed to balance the scales of justice.

My street buddies, Sonny Boy and BooBoo, did a burglary of a doctor's office in Phenix City and got caught. I took the rap for those two and was taken to the county jail in Phenix City. After a few days in jail, a court-appointed lawyer came to see me. He was black, and that's why I trusted him. I explained to him that I had nothing to do with the crime, but he said that didn't matter. He said that I was going to prison because the district attorney said I had been stealing everything not nailed down ever since the days of Adam and Eve.

Well, he was exaggerating a bit, because I only turned eighteen in that county jail. But he advised me that I should confess to the crime and that way I would get a lighter sentence than if I tried to fight the charge (and lost). Either way, I was going to prison. I trusted him—after all, I had no friends or family left in my life—and I looked up to him. But he turned out to be a snake, because I received four years in prison—a heavy sentence—for confessing to a crime I didn't commit.

The county jail was a new experience. I was in with a few homeboys, and they were full of lies and tricks. Movies and TV often focus on prison as the environment for violence, rape, and destruction, but county jails are strong training areas for prison. That's where prisoners learn the art of survival in a confined and dangerous area.

In the county jail, I befriended a man I knew growing up, and that gave me some protection. We agreed to defend each other, and he followed through. In prison or in county jail, you have to fight and have no fear of the next guy in your cell, regardless of his size or reputation. I had no money, no friends, and no visitors. I was in there on my own. I would fight at the least aggravation. I was bigger than most guys, and God has given me the ability not to be afraid in tough situations. My time in the county jail prepared me to step inside the prison door.

In prison, like in the business world, the first minute is crucial to establishing yourself. In fact, that is doubly true in the prison world. When you walk into a prison for the first time, all eyes are on you. You have weak guys, strong guys, and crazy guys all looking at you in order to place you into one of these categories.

I was a street kid, living by my wits. So the way I handled myself, the face I put on, was that of a tough guy. I showed no fear and practically dared anyone to challenge me. Sure enough, I got challenged twice in my first week, and I won the fights both times. After that, I was "established." Once I was established, I ran with guys like me. If you were tough enough—and I was—you could stand in front of the prison store with a bag open, asking guys to drop items in the bag for you. They would do it, too, because they were afraid of you.

On the surface, then, I seemed well adapted to prison life. But I wasn't. Unlike the other guys, I had no friends outside, no phone calls, and no mail. I never received a visit. I wanted a family so bad, and I wanted all the concern and love for me that would have come with it. Because I didn't have that, I was angry at the world and eager to fight.

I especially hated the guys who had families in their lives—a mother and father to visit them. One of my closest friends in prison, Rudy, was a tough street guy like me. I had been on my own since age sixteen, and he had been alone since age fifteen. We could really relate to each other, and we privately talked about it.

On visiting days, we often stood in the window and looked out at the prison's visiting yard. We watched the families visiting our fellow prisoners and tried to imagine what they were saying to one another. We invented conversations. Family members were allowed to bring food, so we would watch them eat and wish we could join them. Not only for the food but for the fellowship, for someone to ask about us and care whether or not we were safe.

Rudy and I challenged each other to pick out the parents we wanted to have. For a mother, I always picked the most beautiful one, and I imagined her caring about me and asking what I had been doing. I never saw a man I wanted as my father. When I wouldn't pick a father, Rudy would get mad and say, "Mitch, you got to pick one." Here he was, a tough guy like me, about six foot three, and he was obsessed with pretending to pick a father from the visiting yard.

Neither of us ever had a visitor, and when other prisoners and guards noticed that, they looked down on us as disposable, throwaway hoodlums. We began to consider ourselves throwaways as well.

7

CHAIN GANG TO PAROLE

After a while, I was transferred to the prison farm to pull weeds. We worked half a day and it was like a chain gang. Keep in mind, chain gangs were legal in Alabama until 1998. We got up before sunrise and headed to the farm. Once we got there, we had to line up for a roll call. Our farm boss was on his horse with his gun, and his assistant would make sure everyone was standing in front of him.

As soon as everyone was in line and accounted for, he would shout, "Start your row!" The row was the area where we would be weeding—pulling coffee weeds. It was hard and taxing work. You can't see any farther than right in front of you. The row is chest high and, early in the morning, very wet with dew. We had no gloves and the weeds had deep roots.

I asked one of the veterans, "What am I supposed to do?"

He laughed and said we had to clear the weeds from around the plant so it could grow. Then he said, "Be sure the weed is not a snake."

I stopped moving and said, "Man, this is crazy." I had to start moving, however, because if I didn't, the guys said the squad boss might shoot me. They were all rednecks who, the prisoners said, would shoot you and tell the authorities you were trying to escape. They might even shoot you for the fun of it.

Sometimes they did yell, "Snake, snake!" for the fun of it. Those in the fields would jump and say, "Where? Where?"

After a while, we became experienced field hands. That coffee weed was hard to pull out of the ground, but I learned that I could pull it out—and save my strength in that sweltering heat—by wrapping the weed around my leg and getting more leverage. Those guards wanted speed, and I was strong enough and tough enough to pull out the coffee weed and not collapse. I could survive the field gangs and the prison, but I still had to admit to myself that my life was worth nothing. No one cared whether I lived, died, or disappeared.

Finally, after twenty months, I was transferred to a level-one prison camp, which meant work release. I was surviving my prison term, and now I could work in society in a regular job alongside people not in prison. At last, I could discard my prison uniform!

My first job was at a steel mill as a small-wheel grinder. My shift was from 3:00 p.m. until 11:00 p.m. I still didn't have any friends or family, and 25 percent of my check went to the state of Alabama. This work-release camp was in a small town, but I requested a transfer to work in a major city. They approved and I went to Montgomery, Alabama. The camp there was larger and had a faster pace. No chain gangs there. After a week or two, I did garbage truck duty and stayed there until I made parole. I went along to get along, but I was not "rehabilitated" in any way. After a while, I went to a halfway house in the same city, and then was released.

8

HALFWAY HOUSE

The halfway house in Montgomery, where I was paroled, was actually located in a nice residential area. Living with ex-cons there was similar to prison. I had to share a room with two other guys. The prison mentality was still alive and well in this environment. On parole, I continued to work on a garbage truck. My routes were in two prosperous areas of town—at least prosperous by my standards—and I marveled at how some people lived.

Everyone in the halfway house neighborhood knew you were an ex-con if you lived there, and the welcome mat wasn't rolled out for you. The man who ran my halfway house was a preacher, who I will call Mr. Blue, and he also ran a loan-shark business on the side. He loaned you money at 25 percent interest.

My best friend in the halfway house was another ex-con named Mickey who was from Mobile. I was twenty and Mickey was about thirty years old. Unfortunately, Mickey would not pay off his loans, but I tried to be on time with my payments. I was determined to be a man of my word on money matters. Mr. Blue showed me some respect when I showed him I could be trusted with money. He liked me and told me I could borrow any amount from him that I wanted because he trusted me.

Mr. Blue told me, however, that he was watching Mickey carefully and didn't trust him. Mr. Blue suggested that I ditch Mickey and said he would be a bad influence on my character. In fact, he told me straight out not to come to him trying to borrow money for Mickey on my name because Mickey was not to be trusted. Well, I did it anyway, but Mr. Blue was right. Mickey didn't pay the money back.

Still, Mr. Blue liked me, and he would ask me to go places with him to pick up rent money. He also told me to get a bank account: start it with $20 a week, he said, and add to it as I prospered. I didn't have a family to support, so he insisted that now was the time for me to accumulate money. I didn't follow his advice, however, because I couldn't read, and that meant I couldn't open an account at a bank. Of course I was ashamed to admit that to Mr. Blue.

Mr. Blue was a mentor to me, and I think he genuinely liked me. One day he let me go with him in his truck to move a person from one of his apartments to a better one. After we did this move, he became very sad, very down in the dumps about something. I asked him what was wrong, and he stopped the truck and asked me to drive for him.

That was a big surprise. Not just because I had no driver's license but because he never let anyone else drive that truck. He even let me take him to his house and see where he lived. I think he was just pretending to be sad to give himself an excuse to let me drive his truck, see his house, and meet his wife. He had a great home and a nice wife, and I was honored that of all the clients at the halfway house, I was the one he helped and let into his life. I had to promise to tell no one where he lived, and I kept that promise.

The next day he wanted to sell me his 1969 Cadillac, which he kept in the driveway at the halfway house and rarely used. This was in 1980, but the car was in fine condition. He told me to give him $300, and I could have it. The car was in good condition with low mileage, so I began saving up for it.

One day I noticed a tall, well-built young lady with a little boy walking up the street by the halfway house. I ran over and introduced myself. She said, "Have you been in prison?"

I said, "Yes," and she said, "For what?"

I said, "For stealing, but I did not do what they said I did."

She said, "You all say that," but she smiled as she said it, and that started our relationship.

Her name was Jamie, and the money I had intended for

the car I gladly spent on her. When Mr. Blue saw what was happening, he said, "Now I know why you have not said anything to me about the car. If you had $300 before, you don't now with a pretty girl like that." What could I say? Soon Jamie and I moved in together with her two kids.

I may have been somewhat effective in street life, but I was incompetent in domestic life. I liked Jamie and wanted to help her two kids, but I didn't do that. The bills took most of my check from my job on the garbage truck. Also, I had to pay $10 per month for being on parole. When I came to work late one day, I got fired, and that stopped my paychecks.

If I was going to be responsible, I had to get another job. I looked carefully, but whenever I found a possible job, I never got it because I couldn't fill out an application because I couldn't read. At one place, Jamie must have put in a word for me. When I went there, the young lady at the desk said she was looking for me. After I told her my name, she said a spot was open for me. I smiled and she said, "All you have to do is fill out the application."

There it was again. The woman gave me the application, and I sat down at the desk, looked at the form, got up, and told her, "I will fill it out and bring it back in an hour."

She said, "Make sure you get it back soon."

Once I stepped outside, I balled up the application and threw it away.

That episode created a big problem because the young lady told Jamie that I refused to turn in the application.

Jamie must have told her I didn't want to work, but just wanted to lie around and let her take care of me, which wasn't true. I was so ashamed of not being able to read that I allowed it to destroy me. I wanted to do the right thing, and I enjoyed the way I was living. But Jamie lost respect for me, and our relationship got to the point where I had to leave.

Then I was in a city without a family, no money, and nowhere to live, not wanting to get back out on the streets. I went to see Mickey. After staying with him three or four days, I decided to leave because I would have to hit the streets once again in order to stay there. I went to Mr. Blue and told him my problems and asked for enough money to get back to Columbus, Georgia. He gave me $100.

Leaving Montgomery meant violating my parole, which meant a warrant was out for my arrest for a parole violation. If and when I was caught, I would have to go back to prison. I couldn't live with my grandmother because that was my last known address. The police were sure to come there looking for me, so I had no home in Columbus even though I had lived there all my life. But I was more comfortable there, even without a home, and I sure didn't want to go back to prison. If I did, I had almost two more years of time to serve. That was a lifetime for a young person, especially since I had just been free again for so short a time.

I was back on the streets once again and back in my old neighborhood, running with the same guys I grew up with.

No one was doing anything positive, and so I was sucked back into the street life.

At least I was on my own, I thought. It was me against the world. The streets were the only things that loved me—they were always there to fall back on.

9

I KILL A MAN

I often say we live a life in a day because of the deci-sions we make throughout that day. December 23, 1980, was the biggest day of my life, and I have lived with that day every day since then. The problem started with pot and alcohol and three of my street friends.

We were hanging out looking for cash and merchandise for Christmas presents. We were on First Avenue in downtown Columbus, Georgia. One of the guys with me saw a nice van. First Avenue back then consisted of regular nightclubs, some strip clubs, regular theaters, and X-rated theaters. After seeing the van parked on First Avenue, one of my street friends named AJ recognized the van and said, "That guy sells drugs. I know him."

Later the man who owned the van came out of the theater. As he was getting into the driver's seat, one member of our group walked up and asked him for a light while another guy walked on the other side with a gun. They got in and hit the horn. Me and the other guy standing on the sidewalk ran and got in the van too. Once we got in, the owner of the van realized that he knew AJ, and he asked him what was going on. I said, "Hey, man, we just want the money and drugs." And we took a small amount of money off of him.

Then we found his pot and cocaine. Two of the guys with me used some of the cain. All of us smoked the pot. We were already just about drunk. We drove across the state line to Phenix City and continued driving until we were on the country roads in Alabama, and then we stopped. The van guy asked, "What's going on?"

AJ said, "Man, you know me. If I let you go, you are going to come back and kill me!"

That is what people do who live that life. If someone is dangerous to you or steals from you too much, you just kill him. We all got out of the van and the van guy was asking AJ not to kill him. AJ was pointing the gun at him, saying, "Man, you know me." It went that way for a minute or two, and we handed the gun around. After a while it landed back in my hands.

AJ said, "Shoot!"

I shot and I did not stop until there were no more bullets in the gun. Five shots.

After the high from the pot and the alcohol was gone and I realized what had happened, I didn't know what to do. It didn't seem real to me. But when it came across the news, I knew it was real!

Then guilt set in. Every time I looked at someone, it was like they were saying to me, "I know what you did!" I was visiting my grandmother's house because it was Christmas, and even she noticed and asked, "Boy, what is wrong with you? You are walking around looking crazy."

Two days after the killing, I came out of the house. The last two nights had been hell. If you have never taken a life, you won't know what I'm talking about. I went into the housing projects and guys I knew were talking about the murder. It was like I was being haunted. I wanted so badly just to tell someone what I'd done. Just to take the pressure off. But I could not.

Let me make two points. First, I didn't think I would get caught. I was sure my three street pals wouldn't snitch. I was wrong. Second, I suffered from constant guilt because I had taken another man's life. Here I was, twenty-one years old. I had committed other crimes, but killing someone was very different. I was weighed down by the guilt of it. Two weeks after the crime, I was caught.

10

JANUARY 6, 1981

January 6 is the date I can truly say my life changed.
On January 5, the day before everything changed, a friend
of mine named Buck 40 had about ten pounds of pot he had
to bag up and sell. He was one of the biggest pot dealers in
my neighborhood. He asked me to help him, so I did. While
we were sitting on the bed, cutting up the pot, I put many of
the big buds off to the side and took them with his blessing.
After we finished, I went to Riverview Apartments, where
my girlfriend, Bella, lived.

Bella was a knockout, a genuine ten, and I can still
recall when I saw her for the first time, walking to the store
in those short pants. All the guys wanted her, but I was the
guy who ended up with her. She was five years older than I
was, and she was a hustler.

When I got to Bella's apartment, she was in the kitchen making banana pudding, my favorite dessert. I had asked her to make it the day before. With the pot more than the pudding on my mind, I asked her, "Where is Willie B.?" Willie, Bella's younger brother, was a fifteen-year-old fellow hustler, and I was going to give him the chance to make some cash with my pot. Willie had no job and was over at his mom's house. I truly thought I was helping him out with my stash of pot. I think sometimes we put ourselves into problem situations where we can no longer escape disaster. That's where I was headed, but I was too blind to see it.

The next morning, January 6, I broke my routine of sleeping until late in the morning. Instead, I woke up at seven and quickly got ready to leave. Bella even said, "Mitch, why are you up so early to leave?"

I said I wanted to get on the corner a little earlier than the other guys who were selling pot. I really had no idea why I got up that early to leave on that particular day. Bella couldn't understand it, and I have trouble with it too.

I went directly to my grandmother's home, but fifty yards from her house I saw a gray car passing her house and coming my way. Being a street kid, I had a sense that the unmarked car was the police, but it passed right by me.

When I got to the front door, my grandmother said the police had come by looking for me. I thought they might be after me for violating parole. Immediately I went into her house, closed the door, and ran to leave from the back. That unmarked car began chasing me. The housing projects are right behind my grandmother's, so I ran into the projects to escape. Why? Because I still had about a pound and a half of pot on me. I saw a doghouse and quickly threw the pot in there. After all, I was on parole, and if I got caught with pot, I would be back doing time. That's where my mind was at the time.

I was running through the projects, and suddenly I was startled to see many police cars coming at me. Men were jumping out of the cars with shotguns. It was early in the morning, so there were not many people about. Seeing all the cars, guns, and police, I started to get scared because I knew they might be inclined to shoot first and ask questions later. And I do mean shoot to kill—I have had police bullets just miss my head in the past, and I didn't want to test anybody's aim this time.

I said to myself, *Mitch, don't make them kill you over a parole violation.* Since I was cornered, I stopped and put my hands up. Three or four officers ran toward me with the shotguns pointed at my head, shouting, "Get on the ground!"

I guess I moved down too slowly, because a cop knocked me down with the butt of his shotgun. Then I felt a boot on my neck, and the man placed the shotgun on the back of my head. I heard a voice say, "Don't you move an inch, scumbag."

No problem. I didn't move a millimeter.

The police handcuffed me and put me in the back of a car. At that moment, I began to realize what was taking place. They asked my name and then drove me to a ranking officer nearby. He ordered me to get out of the car, and as I stood there, he began reading me my rights. After that, he said, "You are being charged with first-degree murder."

My heart almost stopped when I heard that.

After I was caught, the police told me what the other guys who had been with me during the shooting had already told them. My so-called friends had said that I was the shooter. I felt so much pressure from the crime that I almost immediately confessed my guilt to the police. Yes, I had shot the man.

Lying in a one-man cell that night, I could rest. I was freed in a small way. Now I could tell others because the police already knew. Telling on myself was not snitching. I still believed in loyalty. But my three street friends apparently did not. They said the police beat them up and made them tell. The police will do that, so I forgave them. That was a night I will never forget.

I lay on the bunk and looked out the window. First-degree murder was the charge. The Columbus police questioned me for more than four hours, and there I was, twenty-one years old, waiting for the police from Phenix City to come and take me away. My life, I thought, was over.

Soon I was transferred to Lee County, Alabama, where the crime had taken place, and I was handcuffed, leg shackled, and grilled for almost nine hours by police. The three guys in the case with me were also in jail and had clearly been beaten up. One of them was urging the police to kill me. While in jail I called Bella. She was hurt, upset, and crying. She told me that only about three minutes after I left her place, Ray—one of my partners in the killing—had called asking for me. Ray had been arrested already and the police were using him to find me. That day was perhaps destined to be my day of judgment. I couldn't escape it.

11

I MEET GOD

There in the county jail, I went through so much mental anguish. I had talked to Bella, but I couldn't reach anyone else. When you get down to it, I had no real friends in my life to reach out to. Even Bella would soon desert me. I was all alone. After three days, a black officer came to me and asked, "Did you know the DA is planning to charge you with capital murder?"

I said, "What is that?"

He looked at me like I was an ignoramus and said, "Young man, that is when they put you in the electric chair if you are found guilty."

I blinked in disbelief. "You mean they are going to kill me?"

"Yes," he said.

I just walked away, stunned.

Then I looked around me. I was in the bullpen, which consisted of a shower and recreation area. But when the jail was crowded, the bullpen became a living area. Actually it was called the bullpen because 90 percent of the time men came there to fight. You can only have one bull in the pen. And men in jail or prison are always trying to prove that they are the bull. If they sense any weakness in another man, they will try to dominate.

After I walked away from the bars, I went back to my area where I had my mat on the floor, and I just lay there looking up, thinking about what the officer had just told me. I wanted to cry, but I couldn't risk doing that in front of the bulls in the pen. I had no family member to reach out to and I was alone, the same way I had felt when my mother passed away.

My crime was blaring out over the TV and was plastered all over the newspapers too. Opelika was a small town and also the county seat of Lee County where I would be tried, so as I sat there in jail, I realized I was a stranger. No one there knew me and I was on my own. The news stated I would be the first capital case in that county in sixty-one years.

After a few days of hearing news reports about the electric chair, I stood up for a guy in the bullpen. He had his mat under one of the tables, and he lay there all day, reading a book. He was nineteen years old, small, and looked very young, and he appeared to have skin cream on his face. He had never been in trouble before. One of the bulls in the pen—a guy who had already spent time in prison and looked about thirty years old—had some ideas for this kid. This fight had been brewing for days, and all of us saw it coming, but in prison or jail, you don't get involved in other people's feuds. If you do, you may be the next target.

I was only twenty-one, but I decided to run a bluff. When the bull was threatening this young guy, I walked over and said, "Hey screwface, don't mess with him anymore."

He said, "I don't care if you are in here for murder. Get out of my way!"

I said, "Don't bother him again—I'm through talking about it," and I walked over to my area in the pen.

Well, he was afraid to take a chance on fighting me because he couldn't be sure he would win—or he might get badly injured even if he did win. You have to think about those kinds of things in jail. I showed no fear, which is what they feed off of in jail and prison. So the bull stayed away from the kid and from me.

Later that night, I crawled under the table with the kid and began to talk with him. He explained that the book he was reading all the time was the Bible.

I asked, "How do you know God is real?"

He said, "My mother told me: if you want to know if God is real, ask Him to touch you."

I was amazed. I didn't know much about the Bible, and I had never prayed. My grandmother had tried to get me to go to church, but anytime I was near a church service, I got sick to my stomach. It was weird.

Well, later that night, once everyone was asleep, I fell on my knees and said, "God, the little dude under the table said his mother said if you want to know if God is real, ask God to touch you. God, I'm asking You to touch me."

That began and ended my first prayer.

Immediately, a beautiful, warm feeling came over me. I couldn't believe what was happening. Actually, I didn't want it to ever end, but it stopped pretty soon. The next night I prayed and that feeling came over me again. I was so surprised. I had finally met God. I prayed and had this experience again on the third night, but after that when I went back I had no special feeling.

God had introduced Himself; now He apparently wanted me to know Him more through the Bible. I couldn't read, but I sure could talk. And I could pray, and that would be how I could communicate with Him.

I prayed for help. "Please help me, God!"

I prayed so hard.

12

AN ANSWERED PRAYER—A LAWYER

A week or so later, I went to my preliminary hearing. The officials told me I was charged with both robbery and murder. Robbery charges I was used to. Murder? No, I wasn't used to that.

"Do you have a lawyer?" the judge asked.

"No," I answered, and the judge asked, "Would you like me to appoint you one?"

"Yes," I said, and about two days later a local lawyer came to see me. Man, I knew I was in trouble when I talked with this guy. He seemed to be a friend of the district attorney, and he had no interest in putting up a serious defense for me. But he was all I had.

A few days later, an officer came to the bullpen and said, "Rutledge, get ready. Your new lawyer wants to see you."

I got dressed, and they handcuffed me and walked me to a room where this new lawyer was waiting to say something to me. As I walked in, I studied him carefully. He looked like he had stepped out of a television screen with a beautiful lady by his side. He was well dressed and good looking. When he spoke, I could tell he was a northerner. He held out his hand and said, "Hi, I'm Dennis Balske. I'm your new lawyer."

I muttered something about some other guy claiming to be my lawyer, and Dennis said something about maybe working with this other guy. The beautiful lady was Dennis's wife, Joni, who was also a lawyer and worked with him on his cases. If being my lawyer was some kind of booby prize, I wanted Dennis to be the winner. Dennis said he wanted my case and that he really wanted to help me. I had my first prayer answered from the God Express.

Dennis told me that the judge had called the Southern Poverty Law Center and said, "A young man up here is really in need of your help."

I learned later that Dennis and Joni had grown up in Cleveland, Ohio, and both had graduated from law school at Ohio State in 1974. The Southern Poverty Law Center was founded as a civil rights law firm in Montgomery, Alabama, in 1971, and Dennis joined the SPLC in 1978. The SPLC lawyers tended to represent blacks who didn't have much of a chance, regardless of how bad their crime was or how bad their background had been. I fit that category.

Dennis was from Ohio, and I'm from the Deep South, and he had trouble understanding what I was saying. It wasn't just an accent problem. At that time I spoke heavy street slang, which those of us on the street used as a regular language. We called it "yang." The rapper Snoop Dogg speaks it often in his songs. Anyway, Dennis said, "Mitch, I can't understand what you are saying. In order for me to help you, we will need to understand each other."

Dennis brought in people to help me enunciate and communicate. For starters, I was moving my hands all over the place when I spoke and it must have been very distracting. Dennis brought in a lady who sat in front of me with a ruler. I was supposed to keep my hands on my knees when I spoke and if I started to wave them around, she would whack my hands with that ruler. That seems almost cruel when I mention it now, but Dennis was trying to get me ready for the trial. His main concern was my ability to get on the witness stand and speak clearly and act in a manner that wouldn't annoy or alienate the jury.

Dennis also wanted me (and him too) to fit into the local culture of Opelika. He wanted us both to have a calm and pleasant demeanor. I had to dress a certain way and conduct myself a certain way during the trial. "It's very important how the jury perceives you, Mitch," Dennis emphasized.

For example, I had a natural frown, which I didn't even know I had. I guess I instinctively frowned because it helped me get my way on the streets. Dennis told me I couldn't look intimidating while sitting in the courtroom. The frown had to go.

After Dennis left, I asked the guys in jail if I frowned. They looked at me like I was crazy and asked me what I was talking about, because everybody in that jail frowned to look as tough as possible. I studied myself in the mirror and decided that I looked more appealing with a smile than a frown. On the street I had needed to intimidate, but in the courtroom I was going to need to look reassuring.

I worked on my demeanor, as Dennis told me to do. I even had some guys in the jail look up the word *demeanor* in the dictionary and explain what it meant. By the way, some guys resented that I had learned a new word and thought I was upstaging them. You have that in prison: some guys can't process information and interpret it sensibly. Here I was trying to avoid being executed, and they were thinking that I was showing off with my new word.

On one level, I didn't care because I was trying to learn about myself and what made me what I was, and this trial was going to be Life 101. But on another level, I was still an argumentative, thin-skinned kid who didn't run from fights. If some prison guy was going to fault me for working on my demeanor, I would show him my real demeanor. And so I got into a fight—which resulted in the jail officials putting me in isolation for two weeks.

13

THE FIRST TRIAL

Dennis was upset with me when he heard the news of my fight. He patiently explained that my character was important in this trial and that getting into a fight reflected on my character and would irritate those who would be passing judgment on whether I would live or die. That got my attention. I hadn't thought about that before, but I was teachable. After two weeks of isolation, I was back in the bullpen, and soon after back in court.

When I first walked into the courtroom, everyone turned to look at me. The looks on their faces seemed to say, *Is he the one we have been waiting for? Is he the one who murdered that man?* Guilt hit me so hard. The judge, from my viewpoint, was going to send me to death row. I was convinced of that just from all their looks.

It is not like in the movies. You are the person who has killed someone. And you need to be punished for it. And the faces of people in the courtroom, including the jury, seemed to ask, *How could a person do such a thing? What type of person is this we are looking at?*

One of the street guys who had been with me when we stole the van and drove to Opelika got up on the witness stand. He told a lot of lies about how we did it and what we were aiming to do. For that testimony, I think he got thirty or thirty-five years when he was put on trial later. I also testified and told the jury I was sorry for what I had done. But that didn't do much good.

With all testimony in, the jury left and deliberated for about two hours. They found me guilty, but the sentencing phase was where I hoped to avoid execution. The jury could consider mitigating circumstances, such as my childhood environment, any physical or mental abuse, and so on. They also could consider my reasoning ability at the time of the crime and my IQ level. The jury was supposed to put these circumstances on the table and then decide what sentence I would receive. When the jury finished its discussions, everyone was brought back into the courtroom, and I stood beside Dennis to hear my sentence read.

The judge said, "Mr. Rutledge, you have been found guilty of capital murder by a jury of your peers. And they determined your sentence should be death. So I hereby sentence you to be electrocuted in the electric chair until you are dead."

And then the judge gave a date for the execution some-time in August.

This was June 15 or 16, and I turned to Dennis with fear in my eyes and asked, "Are they going to kill me in two months?"

He said no, that I would receive an automatic appeal. I didn't know how long I had because of the automatic appeal, but at least I knew it wouldn't be August.

14

HOLMAN PRISON

On June 17, an officer came to the front of the bars and called out, "Mitchell Rutledge, front and center!"

I made my way up and said, "Here I am."

The jailer said, "Pack up. You are being transferred to death row."

Hearing those words brought great fear upon me. *Death row.*

When the guys in the bullpen heard those words, the room became completely still, no sound at all. It was as though I was the grim reaper of death himself. All the guys looked at me while I got packed. Actually I had very little to pack. After I got downstairs, the desk officer said I could call my family, but I had no family to call. Other than

Dennis, no one called or visited me. I was completely alone.

Next, the prison officials put me in leg shackles and tied me around the waist with the belly chain. Then I was hand-cuffed to that chain and they walked me to the police car. June 17, 1981, age twenty-one. There I was on Interstate 65 South, headed for death row.

I had to get a grip on my emotions. Would I be locked away in some dark area with madmen and killers? Holman Prison was nicknamed "the bottom" in part because it is the prison farthest south in Alabama, at the bottom of the state; but also in part because Holman is the last stop, the bottom, where the incorrigibles are sent. Holman gets those who are too violent for other prisons. It is also the place in Alabama where those sentenced to death are executed.

Thoughts about all this, and my soon-to-be death, filled my head. Two hours or so later, we turned right onto a small paved road that soon became a gravel road. The officers said, "We are here at Holman Prison."

The officers drove up to the tower outside the prison where the prison guards had the checkpoint. Later I learned that inmates call it the back gate. The officers in the tower lowered a basket for the men to check their guns. I watched it all from the backseat. After checking in, a big ramp raised up, and the first gate opened and then shut after we were inside. Finally we got out of the car, and I was inside Holman Prison.

I could see the tag plant and the metal-fabricating area—I learned that they made license plates and also tables, beds, and metal items for prisons and jails in Alabama. Then I was taken to the receiving area to be processed and turned over to Holman officers. The two policemen who had accompanied me from Opelika turned me over to the Holman officials and said, "He is yours now."

The Holman officer then took me on a long walk. "Clear the halls!" he shouted, and I heard doors closing.

That's how I began my walk to death row. Guys were hanging on the bars in the area close to the hall. It was summertime, and most inmates had their shirts off. They stared at me and I stared back. Many guys had scars all over their bodies, which I later learned were from knife wounds—mostly inflicted in prison.

I had been in prison before, but not like this. This was like descending into hell. And this hell was very noisy. My long walk led me to a cell, and I was shut into a room eight by five feet long, with a small bed, a sink, and a table. I could see already that my life was over if God did not intervene.

As I surveyed my new home, I noticed there was no toilet. I hit the wall and heard a guy respond. I said, "Hey man, where's the can?"

He said, "In that hole in the middle of the block," and began to laugh. Sure enough, there was a hole in the middle of a cement block below me.

The guy behind the wall asked where I was from, and I said I was arrested in Opelika in Lee County. He said, "I'm from Magic City," which is Birmingham.

I said, "I'm Mitch," and he said, "Call me Swamp Bear."

I stopped being friendly at that point. Here I am in death row, and I'm next door to Swamp Bear. I thought back to my car ride. Yeah, prison was a dark place, and I'm in a cage next to some beast. Here I am, twenty-one years old, living in the greatest country on earth, and I am in this dark cell with guys nearby like Swamp Bear and, as I would soon discover, Black Jack, Wolf, Mud Dog, and Jungle Bear. I was scared to death. Was my life over?

As time went on, I began to understand more of my new world, which was an eight-foot-long, five-foot-wide cage that was referred to as "the dead end" inside a state prison. After about one month, I knew the guys on my tier, but never to the point that I could call one of them my friend. I never could make a judgment on what decision they would make in this or that situation. I just knew them by voice, name, and face. It was the same way with the officers.

Most of the officers were rural white males. No education was required for their jobs, only the willingness to beat someone if the need arose. And yes, a lot of that took place. Most of the guys in prison with me, black or white, came from the inner city. There was a cultural problem between guards and prisoners, especially with black prisoners. That was important because anytime you needed outside help you had to go through the guards to get it done.

On death row, we could communicate with each other through a "kite," which was a written note passed from cell to cell until it reached the person it was supposed to go to. If the note contained something private, then you glued it up. You could also pass a message down by word of mouth, which would travel cell to cell until it reached its destination. If the message was strictly private, you would wait until shower time and tell the person face-to-face.

Some guys on death row didn't like each other, and there was a hierarchy among us. At the bottom were guys convicted of rape and guys who hurt children or old people. They had little credibility and were looked down on. Sometimes a person low on that hierarchy could gain esteem through physical strength and intimidating people or by good interpersonal relations. That is, if he could communicate effectively and without conflict. Then he could get a little more respect in the prison world.

Prisoners also had varying levels of respect for the officers. Some of the officers had some sympathy for your situation in prison; others treated you exactly the way you treated them; still others thought you had no right to live. All this was part of prison life, and I had to learn it as quickly as possible if I hoped to survive long enough to see execution day.

NOISE

by Mitchell Rutledge
Death Row, Holman Prison
November 11, 1983

> There is so much noise here on death row
> Sometimes you can't hear yourself think.

You have the guy talking,
The TV running,
The radio playing.
The guys talk about everything.
They talk about the law,
Different things that have gone on in their
    lives,
And things that go on around here.
You would not want to hear
Some of the words said around here.
But when you get a whole lot of guys together
You can look for that.

15

I MEET SWAMP BEAR

At first I had very little appetite for food because I was under so much stress. My life was none too good as a teenager, but here I was at age twenty-one, living in a country that taught you that with hard work you could achieve your dreams, and I was living permanently in a cage smaller than most people's closets, on death row with a neighbor named Swamp Bear.

Anyway, with my lack of appetite, Swamp Bear took my food and gladly ate it. One day the officer came by to pass the food trays under the small tray openings in our doors, and when he came to my door, Swamp Bear said, "Put it over here."

I knew right then and there that I had to stop that. I

couldn't allow Swamp Bear to take my food unless I made the decision to give it to him. Otherwise, I was showing weakness, which I knew would create more problems for me. Death row prisoners feed on weakness. So I responded quickly by saying, "Hey Swamp, if I don't give you my tray, don't ask for it." And I left it like that. I said it loud enough for the other guys to hear.

By doing it that way, the word began to get around, "Hey, Mitch will stand up for himself." In a sense, that confident move toward Swamp Bear was my first successful maneuver in establishing myself in my new world of prison. Gradually, I began to look forward to the meals, and I was even eyeing Swamp Bear's tray.

Being confined twenty-three hours and fifteen minutes each day gave me a chance to think. Those meals were all we got, and there wasn't much substance or taste to them. Even with that food, most of us were regularly hungry. Lunch was small, and there was a big time gap between dinner and breakfast. If you had access to outside money, you could get extra food at the prison store. Some guys had that, but I had no family in the area, or at least no one left who cared about me. I was alone and would survive, or not, depending on my ability to make it in my new environment.

You had to be careful in prison about asking for help. Sure, some guys would give you some extra food or maybe do a favor for you. But it was always with the expectation that something would be given in return. If you couldn't give something tangible—food, money, cigarettes—then you would have to give your body. We had no women in prison, of course, and homosexuality was all around. If you had someone doing you favors, that implies to many prisoners you wanted to be taken care of—like a woman.

You were expected to be a woman for that person. All this was part of prison life, and you had to be quick to learn and slow to ask favors. Or you would become a woman in some man's life. Our world was a different world; so much was turned around from the normal outside world.

All of us, however, need some companionship, someone we can talk with and someone who cares about us. I didn't have that in the outside world, and finding any of it inside prison was obviously going to be challenging. People played mind games and tricks with you. I was on guard against anyone who was becoming too friendly with me, even though I was hungry for friendship.

I learned a lot from Swamp Bear, but when I talked with him I had to appear to be conversational and not trying to get a lot of information out of him. If I appeared too green, he would have taken advantage of that in some way. You develop a reputation. Guys sent messages up and down the cells, and some of those messages were intended in part or in whole for you but were not directed personally toward you. Guys were trying to see what they could get away with and how they might be able to use you to their advantage.

They might talk about fights they were in, money they have, or who they like or dislike in prison. Much of this is a game, and I was trying to learn the rules as quickly as possible. Guys were either pushovers or the ones who did the pushing. I was determined not to be a pushover.

Yeah, my spirits were low, but I had to stay focused. I learned how to pray and talk with God. Even though I couldn't read the Bible, I began to relate to some of the biblical characters. I had heard someone read Job 3:1–12 when I was a little kid, and I completely connected with those words: "May the day of my birth perish." Verse 11 says, "Why did I not perish at birth, and die as I came from the womb?"

I wondered why. Maybe there was still a purpose to my life. Maybe I had things yet that God wanted me to accomplish. If so, what were those things? I had a lot to think about as I adjusted to my new life.

POEM

by Mitchell Rutledge
Death Row, Holman Prison
February 21, 1985

> I really don't know
> How in the world
> I got myself
> In all of this trouble
> I'm in now . . .
> I would guess that
> Sounds pretty crazy to you . . .
> But it's true.

16

DEATH ROW

In prison, I was very upset with how my life had turned out. Reflecting back on my life from birth up to age twenty-one, I only saw hardship and pain. Job chapter 11 was something I could truly relate to.

As time went on, I became a regular part of death row life. Surviving on the row without any real outside relationships was difficult. No visits and no mail. Other than Dennis, my lawyer, outside contact wasn't any part of my life for the first year and nine months. I didn't have anyone to say, "I love you, I miss you," and so on. True, that was also the case when I was sixteen (except for the death row part), but this time I didn't take the negative and self-destructive route. I reached out to God.

For the first time in my life, I asked for a Bible. I couldn't read or write, but I did know most of the letters of the alphabet and the sounds they made. With that small beginning, I asked God to help me read the Bible, and every chance I got I would ask someone to read the Bible to me. I followed along as the person read, and I tried to remember the words I heard. Then when I was alone in my cell, I would open the Bible back to where I had it and "read" the words that I remembered.

My memory was always very good, which had helped me many times before I was in prison. Just as a blind person often has a great sense of hearing, I had developed a really good memory when I heard things. Growing up I had to remember details because I never wrote things down. My memory was a big help in finally learning to read and write.

We were allowed to leave our cells for forty-five minutes each day when we could walk, handcuffed in back, in a small area. We were also allowed to go to the Law Library once a week. That is where some guys did legal work and talked legal issues. Other guys played cards, talked with each other, or sometimes fought. If inmates had issues with each other in the cells, they would fight in the Law Library. I went there, however, to try to have someone read the Bible to me.

As time went on, I was able to read the Bible by recalling the words I remembered from the reading. I would also—with my limited literacy—write each word down. That was my foundation for learning different words.

Also, I used television. Death row inmates were allowed to watch television on the stands along the hallway outside of the cells. There were six stands strategically placed for each of the guys in the fourteen cells to be able to view one of the TVs. As I watched TV, every time there were any commercials on, I would watch the words that were placed up there for each item in the commercial.

Detergent was an interesting word. I had pen and paper, and I would write the letters down the best I could and then sound out the letters and associate the word with the item. *Toothpaste* was actually made of two words put together. I didn't know that before. *Toilet paper* taught me about *t*'s and *p*'s. *Aspirin* was a white pill I had taken when I was a kid, but I had no idea how to spell it until prison.

Watching TV was about the only thing to do, and it gave us a distraction to take our minds off the conditions on death row. I often killed fifteen to twenty cockroaches a day in my cell. I would be lying down on my bed and maybe see two or three on the wall and another two or three on the floor. People could go crazy living in conditions like that. The TV helped a lot and was a big deal to us.

The guys closest to the TV had long rods that could change the channels. Those guys had control of the TVs, and we had to watch what they wanted. The person closest to my TV was "The Godfather," so called because he supposedly killed a prison officer in about 1974 while doing time in Alabama. He and I had problems.

For example, sometimes he would change channels in

the middle of a show he knew I was enjoying. Other times, if there was a show coming on he knew I liked, he would turn the TV to channel 2, which was a blank screen. If I asked him why he did that, he would say he wanted to rest and not be bothered by the noise.

Keep in mind I was a very new Christian, and Bible ideas had not taken much root yet in my life. One day, knowing that I wanted to watch television, he turned to channel 2. I said to myself, *That is the last straw.* I told him the next chance I got, when I was allowed my forty-five-minute break to exercise and shower, I would knock his TV off the stand and break it. That way he couldn't control it or me.

When I said that, he responded, "You do that and I'll kill you!"

I threatened him right back that I would beat him up. I was twenty-two years old, six foot three, and 215 pounds— no fat on me. He was forty-one and seemed ancient to me.

When break time came and we went to the shower, I decided against breaking the TV. I had cooled off and wasn't upset anymore; also, I didn't want to ruin my own entertainment just to ruin his. The guards would have been very slow to replace that TV. Also, I knew he would fight, and that would mean one of us would probably die. I didn't want it to be me.

But we had a confrontation anyway because we both ended up in the Law Library on the day when that option was available. It was a tense moment when the guard locked the door to the Law Library. The other guys knew there had been trouble between us, and I figured he had his knife with him. We stared at each other and walked toward each other. He had his hand in his pocket, so I didn't want to be too provocative. But I had to establish my ground in this new prison environment.

The good news is that he didn't want to go to war with me either, so we discussed our issues and reached sort of an understanding about the TV. I say "sort of an understanding" because he would still turn it to channel 2 from time to time, but not as often and not so disrespectfully. Respect is important in prison, and I won some degree of respect from him, so he usually let me watch shows until they were over.

After living next door to him for about a year, our relationship improved and he no longer used the TV to harass me. He and I, like other prisoners, would stand at the bars of our cells and talk for hours about life. We lived next to each other for three years, and during that time he began to open up to me about his life, his experiences, and how he had not killed that prison officer. I was like a little kid waiting to hear more of his grand tale.

RAIN

by Mitchell Rutledge
Death Row, Holman Prison
January 10, 1986

It have been raining ever since yesterday.

DEATH ROW

As you already know,
We don't walk when it's raining.
That mean we have to be in the cell
All day.
I hope it don't be raining tomorrow.
Well tonight is shower night.
I will get out of this box
For about 15 minutes.
Say, do you like it when it rain?

17

LEARNING TO READ

During those years, even though I was sentenced to die, I was preparing to live. Reading was the key, and I was determined to learn to read. As I said before, I learned words by sound and sight. My ability to recall letters and sounds began to improve—I hadn't harmed my mind too much by using drugs on the street. Some of the guys answered my questions about letters and sounds, but mostly I worked by myself, slowly and methodically. I wanted so much to communicate with the outside world—to talk to someone out there and let them know where I was, that I was still alive, and that I wanted a human touch. I prayed to God for a friend, someone who would care about me. But how would I ever find one?

I couldn't write a letter, so I tried to make phone calls. We were allowed one three-minute phone call each month. The procedure was that the guard would call out your name and if you wanted to try a phone call, you would get in a line. When your turn came, you would tell the officer the phone number and he would dial it. The officer dialed my number to call Bella, my ex-girlfriend, and no one answered. That ended my monthly call.

I was so desperate for help, but I couldn't even spell *help* to ask anyone for it. When the officer closed my prison door that night, I felt a sense of panic. I was alone, trapped, surrounded by criminals, and sentenced to die. But I couldn't call anyone or even write *help*. And if I did learn that word, who would I send it to?

I was allowed paper, but I couldn't communicate with it. I couldn't ask a fellow prisoner to write for me, because they often played mind games and wrote whatever they wanted on the paper.

I just had to learn to write. I used my paper to write down letters and connect them with sounds. As I said, I copied words that popped up on television ads. I copied them down and worked on the sounds. I also tried to memorize words. I would look over my list of accumulated words and ask God to help me learn to read. I might or might not survive death row, but I was going to die literate, or at least die trying.

During the day, I would do physical exercise in my cell and then study. I would pick up the Bible each day, trying to learn new words by sounding them out. "God, please help me understand what You are saying here," I would ask, and I continued to get better. I would spell out words in the Bible and ask the guys in the cells next to me what the words were. I would try to comprehend whole sentences this way.

After a while, the guys nearby pretended they were asleep to avoid answering so many questions. Sometimes I would just hold that Bible, wanting to understand it and wanting to read it so badly. With time, I actually began to learn whole sentences.

READING 'N' WRITING

by Mitchell Rutledge
Death Row, Holman Prison
March 7, 1985

> *You know every time I realize*
> *That I am sitting down writing a letter,*
> *I can't believe I'm doing it.*
> *Or when I'm reading something*
> *I'll stop and smile.*
> *It isn't much, but it's more*
> *Than I ever thought I would be able to do.*
> *Before I came to death row I couldn't spell*
> *"The" or "that" or "some" or "help."*
> *All the simple little words like that.*

Listen to me, they are simple now.
But if someone say they can't spell "that" or
    "help"
I would understand
Because I have been there before.
But I will also tell them
With a little hard work they can learn.
It won't be easy but you can do it
Because I was once like you and I did it!

PACK OF COOKIES

by Mitchell Rutledge
Death Row, Holman Prison
March 2, 1986

Today is Sunday.
We don't eat but two times today,
Which mean if you don't have anything
From the store to eat in your cell,
You are in trouble.
Would you believe, I have been trying
To get a pack of cookies all day
For 8 stamps?
Well I have.
I guess no one need any stamps.

18

TIME INTERVIEW

During 1983, *Time* magazine was doing a story on crime and punishment, and they were interviewing death row inmates throughout the United States. When they got to Alabama, they asked the Southern Poverty Law Center to recommend an inmate to interview, and the center chose me. Other inmates on death row told me not to do the interview, but I decided it was a good opportunity.

The person from *Time* magazine came to Holman and interviewed me on the visiting yard. She was a young white lady who looked to be in her late twenties or early thirties. She smoked, and she asked me if I smoked. I said I had just stopped. She began to smoke.

Believe it or not, I cannot remember much of what she

asked me, other than what it was like to be on death row. I guess I was nervous. I said I felt like a dog in a dog pen waiting to die. Then she also asked me if I was sorry for my actions and if I had remorse.

I said yes and explained why. That's all I remember.

After I did the interview and the article came out, the guys on death row immediately began ridiculing me. Why? Because *Time* magazine reported that convicted murderer Mitchell Rutledge had an IQ of 84, just barely above mental retardation. The article also said I never had any visitors (except for my court-appointed lawyer). The conclusion the writer made was that since I was obviously mentally defective and was of no value to anyone, I should just be locked up forever and let's be done with it. "Forget him" were the last words.

My fellow prisoners were laughing at me, and I had to admit that I had scored poorly on the prison's mental evaluation because I couldn't read. The article portrayed me as worthless and almost subhuman—hardly a grand entrance for my opening communication to the outside world. But what I was about to see was the movement of God. If He could make a donkey talk and then make the sun stand still for Joshua, He could put that article to use for me, and that's exactly what happened.

19

NEW FRIENDS—AT LAST!

LILLIAN'S STORY

I am a teacher, and when I read the section in the *Time* article featuring Mitchell Rutledge, it was on a school morning. I lived in Southern California, where I had grown up and gone to college. My schedule on such a morning was tight and measured to arrive at school on time. But that morning I did what I felt compelled to do regardless of the time constraint.

Several points struck me as I read the passage: Mitchell's age, his admission of guilt and remorse, and his realization that his expressing regret would not be understood. When the interviewer labeled Mitchell with a low IQ score, my strong adverse reaction was that this resulted in denigrating Mitchell's worth as a person. But the words "not worth killing" were the most offensive I had read about a human being. That statement completely negated every humanitarian principle I held. What concept, when you think about it, would be more annihilating to a person's value!

The journalist's next suggestion followed, "Let him sit in his eight-by-five-foot cell and forget him . . ."[1]

This caused a quotation from the book of Isaiah to surface in my memory: "I will not forget you! See, I have engraved you on the palms of my hands," says the Lord (Isa. 49:15–16).

The very next moment, I wrote my response to *Time*, objecting to the educationally unethical use of an IQ score and their negative characterization of Mitchell as a human being "not worth killing." I stated this was one person who would not forget him and said they could forward my letter to him, which they did.

BURT'S STORY

I was teaching history at Murray State University in Kentucky when my wife, Anita, and I read the *Time* article. The death penalty was hotly debated in those days because the federal case involving inmate Gary Gilmore and the death penalty had been in the news. The *Time* article was lengthy and covered the details of many prisoners. Anita and I were so saddened by the tragic stories of the heinous murders committed by the men who were now sitting on death row in various prisons around the country.

These accounts of murder and death row prisoners were foreign to my background. Many of the inmates were African Americans. I grew up in the suburbs of Lincoln, Nebraska, and I knew few blacks growing up. I did study black history in college, but it was just an area of study I needed to cover to get my PhD in American economic history.

I was glad when the Supreme Court restored the death penalty in the 1980s, because execution seemed to me to be the proper penalty for premeditated murder. When I came to the Mitchell Rutledge story, however, I was stumped. This Mitchell Rutledge was the only person in the article who said he was sorry for his crime and that he regretted what he had done. I was also struck by the statement that he never had visitors other than his lawyer. I had only been a Christian for one year, and I wondered if this Rutledge guy might be executed before he had a chance to know that God would forgive him, that he could go to heaven if he accepted Jesus into his life.

I went to bed that night, but I couldn't sleep because I kept thinking of that prisoner on death row in Alabama. I couldn't get him out of my mind. Was this guy with the 84 IQ capable of reading a letter and understanding the salvation message? The next day, I wrote a letter in block letters to Mitchell Rutledge, telling him who I was and that I wanted to correspond with him.

I said that I had read his article in *Time*, and I told him, "What you did was wrong, but you are right to say you're sorry for what you did. You can accept God's forgiveness and even if you are executed, you can go to heaven."

I didn't have an address in Alabama. The atlas I looked at showed no town of Holman in Alabama, so I simply wrote "Holman Prison, Alabama" under Mitchell's name and picked out a zip code in Alabama. Then I prayed that he would receive my letter and I mailed it.

When I told Anita what I had done, she was fine that I had written the inmate but she wasn't confident that he would ever receive it. "You just picked out a zip code? The post office wouldn't even deliver my letter to my mother last week when I accidentally had one number wrong in the address. My letter came back. How is that guy going to get the letter when the zip code is totally wrong?" she asked.

But miraculously, Mitch did get my letter.

20

JOHN LOUIS EVANS III

These friends, Lillian and Burt, came none too soon.
The laws on capital punishment were changing, and the US
Supreme Court upheld the death penalty under certain circumstances. That meant that if states wanted to, they could
begin executing prisoners who were on death row. When
the state of Alabama changed its law and instituted capital
punishment, all of us on death row were suddenly subject
to execution. That's when the death marches in Alabama
began.

The first guy to be executed was John Louis Evans III. I
knew John because he was our hall runner. We didn't have
hall runners when I first came to death row, but we did
now because we needed someone during the day to bring

information, or even grievances, to the attention of officers. Otherwise, some prisoner might die in his cell, or might be too sick to move, and no one might notice for a long time. Or some prisoner might throw feces or urine on you, and you'd need something to clean it up. Or perhaps a prisoner received an urgent letter from home and needed to make an emergency phone call. The hall runner could help you with that.

John and I were on the same side of the prison. He was in 7-D and I was in 7-U—we had fourteen men to a tier and twenty-eight men on the 7 side. I looked up to John. His long criminal record had given him a national reputation, and he had a strong legal team behind him. CBS later made a movie out of his life, and I was pleased that he was our hall runner, the guy who could relay a serious and urgent need to the officers.

John was in his early thirties, a white man, loved sharing stories, and had a fun sense of humor. For example, I often shadowboxed in my cell for exercise. When he first walked by my cell, he imitated me and began shadowboxing, and he did so with a big grin on his face. The first two or three times he came by my cell, he shadowboxed with me, but only briefly and then he moved on. After a while, he shadowboxed with me and wouldn't stop until I stopped. I mean, this would go on for minutes at a time, so I said, "Are you crazy?" and he echoed right back, "Are you crazy?" I asked, "Do you have a problem?" and he repeated my words back to me.

I dismissed him, but the next day he came by and asked, "Mitch, can you really box?"

I said, "No, it's only exercise for me," and he said, "I thought so," and smiled and walked off. I smiled, too, because we had made a connection.

John would tell me and others lots of stories, and he fancied himself a clever outlaw. He did get away with thirty robberies, but then he and his partner killed a pawnbroker in Mobile. John was smart and escaped the police. But then he called them, and the FBI, to taunt them for not catching him. Well, they eventually did catch him and put him in Holman.

He told me he didn't believe he would be executed, and he fought hard to stop it from happening. As the date of his execution came closer, I could see the fear in his eyes. In Holman, executions were scheduled for Fridays at 12:01 a.m. They took you to the death cell on the Monday morning before your execution, and you would stay there until they took you to the electric chair.

One Monday I heard that John had been taken to the death cell, and my whole life suddenly came into context. The electric chair—some inmates called it "the Yellow Mama"—wasn't that far from death row. I had looked at it once, but I never wanted to see it again. Some of the guys on my tier had even sat in the chair when they were out of their cells! Not me.

During the week, John was nowhere to be seen and on that Thursday night, April 21, 1983, he waited to be executed. Even though he received a "stay" of a few hours, he was executed that Friday. And all the prisoners in Holman, those on death row and in the general population, knew it was happening. When he was electrocuted, suddenly we could smell burning flesh and hair. It was nauseating. But the first jolt from the Yellow Mama didn't kill him, so they gave him another. Again the stench of burning flesh continued.

A lot of the prisoners began hitting the bars on their cells with anything that would make a noise. That would become a tradition during later executions. But John Evans was still alive. Then came a third jolt, and that killed him. After three jolts and fourteen minutes, John Louis Evans III became the first of a long line of prisoners on death row in Alabama to visit the Yellow Mama. If it could happen to an articulate and well-connected guy like John, with a caring family and a prominent lawyer, what chance would I have?

My life on death row was unpleasant in so many ways, but also it was probably going to be short unless something unusual occurred. I say short because I had admitted my crime. Therefore, I was automatically guilty and subject to the death penalty. Others who were being executed had proclaimed their innocence, but they were executed anyway. At least they had the chance to appeal their sentence.

Since I had confessed my guilt, in the eyes of the law I had no chance to go free. Dennis's best possible result would be to get me off death row to life without parole. And even that seemed impossible. Others, with more influence and better arguments than I had, were failing one after another to get off of death row.

BEING KILLED

by Mitchell Rutledge
Death Row, Holman Prison
1985

> *For every minute I spend on death row*
> *I realize that I stand a very good chance*
> *Of being killed.*
> *I never forget that.*
> *But I don't think I could make it*
> *Sitting up here thinking about dying*
> *Every day.*

21

GETTING TO KNOW MY NEW FRIENDS

I received the letters from Lillian in California and from the college professor in Kentucky. As it turned out, Lillian was not only a teacher but also a Catholic sister, and she had very strong feelings against the death penalty. She asked me to call her "Sister Lillian." A housewife from Virginia named Pam also wrote to me by sending her letter to *Time* and asking them to forward it. Pam was as outraged as Lillian had been about what the reporter had said about me: that perhaps I should be locked in a cell and forgotten, that I was not even worth executing. I was so glad to get those letters.

I was barely literate, but I had to respond. I asked the guy in the next cell to read their letters to me. When he read the letters, I memorized what they were saying. I would then repeat some of their words in my response to them and would also go to my list of words that I was learning to see if any of those words would be usable. I would also add some of the words being written to me to that list. I labored diligently over those letters, and I prayed and read the Bible while I worked on them.

All three of my new friends responded to my letters, so I went through the process again with the inmate in the next cell reading their letters to me. By the way, I never let him see any addresses on the letters because I couldn't have him, or anyone else, write them and interfere with what I was doing.

I was very nervous every time I sent the letters, worried that they wouldn't write me back, and I had to build my friendships with them one letter at a time. In 1984, after doing this for about one year, I discovered that I could read my own letters now. I was so excited—I could actually read and write letters to my new friends! True, they were writing simple letters and helping me along, but I was getting better month by month.

LETTER TO LILLIAN

by Mitchell Rutledge
Death Row, Holman Prison
July 1983

> *I have did a whole lot of things*
> *That you have not did.*

But you have did a whole lot of things
That I have not did.
And the things that I have did,
I know that you don't want to do them.
But all the things that you have did,
I would like to have a chance
To do some of them.

ANITA'S STORY

Burt and I were surprised but very happy to get a letter back from Mitch in response to the first letter that Burt had written. Yes, the zip code and the address hadn't been accurate, and Burt's first letter didn't even have Mitch's inmate number on the envelope. But someone in Holman Prison must have been led by the Lord to overlook that, and he or she sent the envelope through to Mitch anyway.

Mitch's sentences in his response were difficult to understand because his writing was still very poor. We guessed at the meaning of some of his expressions, and this time we sent him another letter using his correct address. Again, in a couple of weeks we had a response from him, telling us more about himself and his life in prison. He printed all his words and his sentences were short.

Our exchange of letters continued throughout 1983 and into the next year. In May 1984, we were planning to drive from Kentucky to Florida to visit Burt's step-grandmother, so we asked Mitch if we could visit him in Holman, and he said yes! He put both our names on his list of approved visitors.

Finally the day came when Burt and I drove up to Holman and parked our car. The prison was a series of long, white, flat-topped buildings, with a huge fence surrounding the entire place. Coils of razor wire were at the top of the fence and guard towers dotted the perimeter. We could see the guards in the tower nearest the parking lot.

We went up to the visitors' gate, and I guess the tower guard buzzed us in. Then we entered the first prison building, which held the visiting yard for guests, and the door clanged shut behind us. We were locked in now. We could only take in our driver's licenses and coins, no paper money. A female guard searched me in the hallway near the women's restroom, and a male guard did the same with Burt in the other room. There were soda machines in the hall and a few snack machines, where visitors could use their coins to buy treats for themselves and the inmates they were visiting.

Then they buzzed us through the security door to the visiting yard, which was a big room with perhaps a dozen square metal tables about the size of card tables, and four stools that were fastened to the floor around each table. The tables were fastened to the floor too. There wasn't anything in the room that someone could pick up and use as a weapon. And there was no air-conditioning.

We sat there for a few minutes, waiting for them to bring

Mitch. Soon a door on the other side of the room opened, and I could see him in handcuffs. One of the guards removed the handcuffs, and in walked Mitchell Rutledge.

My first impression was that he was a really big man, very powerful looking, and my second thought was that I could see he was terribly nervous. I didn't laugh, but I thought that was hilarious. I kept thinking, *Why is he nervous? We should be the ones who are nervous!*

We shook hands and all sat down for our first face-to-face conversation. The *Time* magazine article had said that Mitch had an IQ of only 84, but as we sat there, we had a very interesting conversation with a young man who was obviously no dummy. I can't remember all we talked about, but I distinctly remember the deep impression that as Mitch, Burt, and I occupied three of the stools around that table, on the fourth stool Jesus was sitting, approving of our conversation and watching the entire meeting. It was a distinct impression of a spiritual event. Although I didn't see the Lord, He was there. I have never had that experience again.

Because Mitch was on death row, his visiting time was separate from the inmates in the general prison population. No one else on death row had visitors that day, so we had the visiting yard to ourselves. We stayed for an hour or two, and then we shook his hand again and told him we would continue to write and we would try to come again.

As Burt and I walked down the sidewalk to our car, Burt's first words were, "That guy is a lot smarter than any 84 IQ."

I agreed.

NOT ALONE

by Mitchell Rutledge
Death Row, Holman Prison
March 3, 1985

> I haven't been up to much
> Trying to keep my head in the right place.
> That's really hard to do sometimes
> Because of the problem that I'm facing.
> But I'm not alone with this problem.
> And when I look around and see
> Other guys facing the same problem
> It's their faith and hope that help me.
> It give me faith and hope
> When I'm feeling down.
> I also give. So it goes the other way also.
> We help each other and don't really realize it.

22

ANOTHER CHANCE

I kept writing my friends on the outside and getting to know them better through my letters. All this was just in time for my new sentencing hearing in 1985. Dennis had been working on that, and it was scheduled for October. I had been convicted of first-degree murder and sentenced to death at the first trial, but now I would have my sentence reviewed. The judge and jury were to decide if I would receive the death penalty or life without parole. Dennis said it was a long shot, but we would try. At Dennis's suggestion, I wrote my new friends about my sentencing and asked if they would be willing to come down as character witnesses for me.

I had met Burt and Anita, but I still hadn't met Lillian

face-to-face because she lived in California. She had attended a high school reunion in 1985 in Santa Monica, California, where she had grown up, and one of her former classmates was now a lawyer. Lillian told him that she might be testifying in a capital murder case, for the defense. The lawyer asked if she'd met me yet. Lillian said no, and the lawyer told her it was very important that she meet me before the sentencing hearing. That would make a much better impression on the jury, the lawyer said.

I was nervous. If any of them came to help me, would they like me after the hearing? Would they believe in me when they heard the district attorney outline my crime with all the details? Would they testify to help me get my sentence reduced to life without parole? I hadn't even met Lillian in person yet.

23

PRISON POLITICS

While I was on death row, I sometimes took part in prison politics. That idea may sound silly, but in prison, just like in any other place, you have issues that come up and different opinions to consider. I understand the view that people in prison shouldn't have it easy. We committed crimes; those of us on death row had even committed murder. Prison was no vacation resort but a place of confinement. I was either to be put to death or sentenced to spend the rest of my life confined in a small area surrounded by dangerous people.

Those of us on death row tried to increase our liberty ever so slightly whenever we could. Prisoners on death row, for example, were by law allowed forty-five-minute walks each day. But those walks occurred in a fifteen-by-ten-foot cage, and we were handcuffed in back. We lobbied to get time on the main yard, the same privilege as those in general population had, but the warden turned us down. He said he couldn't spare the officers to guard all of us if we were allowed to do those walks. The possible intermingling of death row with general population might allow drugs to be transferred, and in any case the death row prisoners required extra supervision, and the warden told us he didn't have the manpower to do it.

The guys on death row made a counterproposal: we will give up the daily forty-five-minute walks, which takes a lot of time for the guards, if you will give us in return three hours once a week without handcuffs in the big yard. That would be one day a week for prison guards, and it would give us a chance to get serious exercise outside our cells, possibly playing basketball in the big yard.

The warden and the officers resisted this request. We even had situations where we were kept in cages with handcuffs on and out in the open sun for one to two hours to break us down. But we continued to protest, and eventually the warden granted us a three-hour visit to the big yard once a week.

The officers did have more difficult duty now, because drugs and contraband could be exchanged through the fence between inmates on death row and those in the general population during these three-hour visits to the big yard.

Also, on death row we won another grievance—to have

our handcuffs removed when we went to the big yard. Granted, this also made extra work for the guards. We were allowed to shower every other day, and when our shower day occurred on the day for our three hours in the big yard, then the guards were very busy. With that much freedom, some fights broke out in the yard, and the officers let that go for the most part. But one day, in a rough basketball game, a troublemaker threw a basketball in the face of a rough guy from my tier—who then tried to kill him for throwing the ball. The guards stepped in to prevent a murder, but that ended our privilege of the three hours in the yard.

I had had trouble with that prisoner before—the one who threw the basketball. He tried to dominate other people on my tier, and he tried to take advantage of me when he could. For example, he was a Dallas Cowboys football fan, and when I was watching a movie on my TV with other guys, he asked if I would change the channel to let him watch one play. I consented. Well, he then wanted to watch two plays, then three. When I changed the TV back to the show I was watching, he threatened to destroy my TV.

I confronted him and told him if he did that, I would make him pay for it. He didn't like hearing that, but he wasn't sure he could dominate me. Remember, I am six foot three and was in great physical shape. I was a Christian, but I believed God wanted me strong physically as well as spiritually. The more respected I was physically, the better I could survive and make the case for God spiritually to my fellow prisoners when the chance came along.

Well, that prisoner wouldn't give up. He was in cell number 7-U-11 and I was in 7-U-12, and he would argue with me to try to dominate me or break me down. Our next misunderstanding came when I said Jesse Jackson was a jackleg preacher, no Martin Luther King for sure. He said black Americans should support their leaders, and I said black leaders should respectfully represent black people and not be out for the money the way Jesse Jackson was. That upset him so much that he began to make a knife. He wanted to kill me, and he prepared for battle.

Here was my problem: Sister Lillian was coming to town soon to see her new reformed friend, and here I was with a guy ready to kill me in a knife fight. I had a visit with Lillian scheduled, and our tier would have its time on the big yard the same day. I could literally have gone from an emotional life-giving meeting with Lillian into a life-or-death knife fight with a madman two minutes later.

I had the meeting with Lillian, and we sat in the visiting yard and talked. It was great to spend time with her, because by then we had been writing back and forth for more than two years.

Then my time with Lillian was over and the guards escorted me off the visiting yard. When I came back, the officer told me my tier had just gone out to the big yard. I could have asked to go back to my cell and postponed the fight, but if I had done that I would have appeared weak. So I asked to go into the yard.

The guard took my handcuffs off, and as I approached

the door, I took my belt off and wrapped it around my hand with the buckle on my knuckles. Then I entered the yard. I shut the door to the yard behind me in case my enemy rushed me. My senses were sharp, and my eyes darted around the yard. I saw the guy near the basketball court talking calmly with other prisoners. I knew them all and walked toward them.

Suddenly, Blackjack, one of the prisoners, came up to me and said, "We talked him down."

I was surprised. "What? Are you sure you have talked that lunatic down?"

Blackjack smiled. "It's over. He has seen you fight before. We talked to him about it, and it's over."

That was a relief.

And even better, Lillian and Burt had both said they would come to testify at my hearing and they would pay for their own travel expenses. Burt and Anita had a new baby, born that summer, and Anita had just gone back to work after maternity leave, so she couldn't come. But I was excited about Lillian and Burt being there and that some of my family members would come and testify too.

I was transported back to Opelika for the hearing. If I got life without parole, I would still be in Holman, but at least I could get off death row and move around inside the prison. I was looking forward to that. And of course, it would mean I wouldn't be executed. That was the best part. But I knew that getting my sentence reduced was a long shot.

HOLDING CELL CONVERSATION

by Mitchell Rutledge, written about a conversation in the
Opelika jail

You know I like talking to people.
I like telling them not to do this or that
Because if you do you will end up like this.
I get a great deal from that.
I really do.
When I was in the county jail for my
   rehearing
There was a guy about 18 or 19 years old.
And they had him in there for rape
And his trial was coming
About the same time my rehearing was.
When you have to go to court they have a cell
That they put you in.
It is called the holding cell.
Me and this guy was in this cell together
Two times.
And I could see that this guy
Was on the same road that I was on about 8
   years ago.
So I started talking to him
About staying out of trouble,
About how to carry yourself
If you go down the road
That mean come to prison.

And I know that I was helping him
If he was listening to anything that I was
   saying
And he was I think.
Because everything I was telling him
I had been through it.
I got something out of that
Just by helping this young guy.
That have help me to learn how you feel
When you have helped someone or try to
   anyway.
It's a beautiful feeling.

24

1985 SENTENCING HEARING

BURT'S STORY

Mitch's sentencing hearing was set for October 1985. I had known Mitch for more than two years and had visited him with Anita. His letters showed steady improvement in grammar and spelling, and that increase in literacy gave his thoughtful mind more room for expression. Mitch learned quickly and was inspiring me in the way he showed character and improved his life day to day.

I wasn't sure what to expect at the sentencing hearing. Mitch had confessed his guilt, and death was the penalty for a capital crime. The only choices the jury had were death or life without parole, which not only seemed remote but also, to me, less desirable. "If you are executed," I told Mitch, "you would go to be with God right away. If you have life without parole, you will be in prison maybe for decades in horrible circumstances. Are you sure you want to go for life without parole?"

Mitch was adamant that he wanted to live and not die. He said he wanted to live with purpose and accomplish something of what God had intended for him. He wanted to grow and learn and live.

I agreed to help Mitch, but I wasn't sure what good I could do. If Mitch wanted me, then I wanted to come. Mitch wanted Anita to come, too, but since she had recently given birth to our son Adam, she had to stay in Murray. I dismissed my college classes and drove to Opelika to support Mitch.

I checked into the motel that Dennis had recommended. I met Sister Lillian, who was excited to be there for Mitch. And I met Dennis. After our introductions, he said, "Mitch is my favorite death row client. This sentencing hearing is a long shot, but it is important to me too."

The next day I spent almost an hour with Dennis and his legal team going over details. We had to show that Mitch was making progress and that his life had meaning to some people. At Dennis's request, I had brought several of Mitch's letters that I thought showed the depth of his thinking and his improvement in expressing himself.

Dennis was always professional, but he worked diligently for the politically left-leaning Southern Poverty Law

Center, and he strongly opposed the death penalty. I'm politically conservative and support the death penalty in some cases, but not in Mitch's. Dennis and I got along well, but our ideas were very different. For example, he privately called Ron Myers, the district attorney, a "country club Republican." My father was a lifelong Republican and the president of our local country club while I was growing up. I didn't at that time feel my competitive juices rising over the face-off with Myers. He seemed reasonable, not diabolical. After all, he was only doing his job as the district attorney.

The sentencing hearing began the next day, and all Mitch's witnesses were cloistered in a room at the courthouse. I met Mitch's two brothers and sister and some other relatives. Aunt Dewbell was my favorite—she was a grand lady, eighty-one years old, and she resonated dignity and grace under pressure. All would testify for Mitch, but so would Mitch's critics—his colleagues in crime and the victim's mother and his widow. The witnesses would go in one at a time—no one would be able to hear any of the trial before he or she testified.

I didn't hear any of the proceedings because I was the last witness. Dennis asked that I go last because he said I would have the most credibility with the jury. It was indeed that desperate. Dennis said that Mitch's family and Sister Lillian could be discounted because of biases, but with my beliefs as a political conservative, I could not be so easily dismissed.

Events in the waiting room added pressure. I had several

of Mitch's letters, which Dennis wanted me to submit to the jury, but I decided to fold those letters and put them in my suit coat pocket in the waiting room. Mitch's family should not see them because in those letters Mitch said he was sad that his family seemed to have deserted him. Lillian, Anita, and I were his new family. I didn't dare let family members, all of whom Dennis had rounded up for the hearing, see those letters before they went in to testify.

When my turn finally came, I walked into the courtroom and the atmosphere was tense. Dennis greeted me and I quickly turned to find Mitch, who was sitting at the defendant table with all the grace he could muster. Dennis was smooth and easygoing as he asked me questions about my growing relationship with Mitch. He then walked over to the jury and asked what Mitch meant to me. That was deliberate so that I would be looking right at the jury as I answered Dennis.

I spoke about Mitch's value as a human being and how I liked watching him improve his abilities and try to make something of his life. I liked Mitch the more I got to know him. He had converted to Christ, and he wanted to follow Him the rest of his life. Mitch could still make a difference in prison if he were allowed to live. Dennis seemed pleased and turned me over to Myers for cross-examination.

Mr. Myers was tall, lean, and dignified. But when he rose to address me, he mixed sarcasm, shouts, and hostile questions. The country club Republican vanished. Dennis was right. This guy was tough. Did I realize what Mitch had done? Did I know his past record of crime and prison? How did I know I wasn't being conned? What about the trail of destruction Mitch had left in this world?

Then he impugned my motives. He seemed to think I was a ringer, some guy Dennis had set up to help him bail out Mitch. Myers was astonished at my political views and challenged me. I was confident he had earlier tried to paint Sister Lillian as a bleeding-heart liberal, but he couldn't do that with me.

I found out later from Dennis that when I gave Mitch's letters to the court, my motel receipt (from my coat pocket) had gotten jumbled into the letters. That gave the impression to Myers that Dennis brought me in at his expense as a personal friend to testify falsely for Mitch. Maybe my letters were a hoax, he thought. When Myers asked if the Southern Poverty Law Center had paid my way, I said no, that Mitch was my friend and I paid my own way and did so gladly. Myers made some disdainful closing remarks and let me go.

I was rattled at what had happened—and at how important my sharp exchange with Myers might be for the jury to consider. Had I helped our cause or hurt it? I left the witness stand and headed toward the back of the courtroom. As I walked past Aunt Dewbell, she reached out her hand and touched my arm. "Thank you for what you just did for us," she said softly, fully upright and with great dignity. Here was a black woman, born in 1904, who had seen much that was wrong about race in Alabama. Her comment to me remains my most vivid memory of the whole trial.

The judge said he would make his decision later. I did get to talk briefly with Mitch, and he thanked all of us for showing up for him. Here he was with the death sentence hanging over him, but he was asking about me and then about Anita and Adam. He told me how much we all meant to him. I said good-bye to Lillian, Dennis, and the relatives.

Shortly thereafter, the judge returned the verdict: death by the electric chair. Was all this for nothing?

THE DAY AFTER THE JURY RETURNED
THE DEATH PENALTY

by Mitchell Rutledge
Opelika, Alabama—Lee County Jail
October 25, 1985

> The days in this place are very long.
> There isn't very much to do.
> I can do much more thinking here
> Because that is all there is to do.
> When you have too much time
> To let your mind open up,
> You begin to think about things
> You shouldn't think about.
> It's very hard sitting back here in this cell
> All by myself with the death sentence given
>   to me the second time.
> That can put all types of ideas into your head.

Now don't go worrying about me hurting
  myself,
Because that haven't came into my mind at
  this time.
And I don't plan on it coming up.
Now lots of people would try to hurt
  themselves,
Because they would feel they have nothing
  else
To live for.
Well that could be said in my case
But I'm not ready to give up on life now.
And I won't be ready until death walk me
  down
And after death have walk me down
If there is any way for me to get up and run
I will do it.

NOT READY

by Mitchell Rutledge
Opelika, Alabama—Lee County Jail
November 5, 1985

I just don't believe God is ready for me.
I really do feel very strongly about that.
I don't know why I feel that way.

Something keep coming in my mind saying
God knows that you have had a hard life,
And have done wrong,
And have to pay for it,
But not with your life.

Because God have something for you to do.
That stay in my head all the time.

I can't tell you why for nothing in this world.
Now I could be wrong about that
Because I have been wrong about many other
    things.

But God is looking out for me.
Why do you think He sent you my way?
You are a part of God's plan that He have
    for me,
And only God know what it is.
See God knows my heart.
God also know that I didn't plan
To kill anyone.
Like I said, I could be wrong about what I
    feel.
We will find out in the future, won't we?

25

BACK IN HOLMAN ON DEATH ROW

My family again deserted me, and who can blame them, given all the bad things I had done? But my new friends Lillian, Burt, Anita, and Pam and her family supported me and wrote me regularly. Also, Lillian, Burt, and Anita began regular visits to the prison. Lillian even arranged for me to get a color TV outside my prison cell, and I told my fellow inmates that if they had any problems with me to take it out on me and not on my new TV.

I remained in my eight-by-five-foot cell with my Bible and my lists of words. But this time I had friends that I knew would stick by me, and that, with God's help, gave me the courage to keep going. Yes, I was scheduled to be executed, but I wasn't alone anymore.

My friends were writing letters of support and letting me make phone calls to them. They also sent me some money so that I could get food from the prison store. The regular food served at meals was often inedible, but at the store I could get better food items, sometimes sandwiches I enjoyed. Best of all they told me they loved me and believed in me. In my entire life, the only family member who ever used the word *love* toward me was Aunt Dewbell.

Looking back, I did know in my heart through smiles and actions that my mom and grandmother loved me, but they just never said so. I received one birthday gift from my mother, a two-piece suit for my sixteenth birthday. It was the last year she was alive. But my new friends were sending me birthday gifts on October 8 and treating me like a family member. Frankly, they were my new family, and all this helped me face death row.

One odd thing here is that my lawyer and my new friends were white, and I am black. I spent my whole life among blacks in black neighborhoods, but my new friends were white. I wasn't taught to hate whites and, in fact, I had some white acquaintances in school. But now my friendships were all with whites. God was using this to broaden my life and show me that love transcends race.

Death row can be a depressing place, but even though I was riding a death sentence, I was alive with energy and anxious to draw closer to God and be a better person. I told other prisoners that God could change hearts and do miracles even in the dark dungeon where we were imprisoned. I was a new man.

I was sent to death row to die, but it became a place where I came alive. Man said I would die there, but God said I would live. With people outside who cared about me, I could face those inside who really cared for no one.

FACING UP

by Mitchell Rutledge
Death Row, Holman Prison
1985

A while back I would tell everyone
That the world was the cause of me being the
  way I was.
And society is the cause of me being in
  prison.
But I don't feel that way now.
I am the cause of me being in prison.
And I was the cause of me being the way I
  was
Because I didn't want to face up
To me and my problems.
I believe that you understand me more than
  anyone else.

I can be Mitch with you.
When I was out there living the street life
I had to be hard and cold.
But that's not really me.
I'm a very caring person, really I am.
The only person who knew that
Was my beautiful mother,
And God.

RAT ON THE LOOSE

by Mitchell Rutledge
Death Row, Holman Prison
November 22, 1985

We are having some trouble with a rat now.
One of the guys said that a rat was in the bed
*   with him the other night.*
I had run one out of my cell about two days
*   ago.*
I think they are just coming back,
Because I haven't seen a rat in a long time,
Until the other day.

26

VISITING MITCH

After Burt and I learned the routine for visiting an inmate in Holman Prison, the process became easier. In the spring of 1986, we spent a few days on the Florida gulf coast and then drove over to Holman.

Mitch was expecting us. He hadn't seen our son, who was by then about eight months old. It had been a long time since Mitch had held a baby, and he was nervous and worried that he might drop Adam when he held him on his lap. But Adam just smiled and put his baby fingers in his mouth, as he usually did.

As time passed, we visited Mitch when we could, but

it was a long trip from Kentucky to southern Alabama. The same female guard I had met during our first visit still escorted me into the visiting yard each time. She was clearly puzzled about why we were there. A white family visiting a black inmate didn't happen every day.

"Are you related to Mr. Rutledge?" she asked one day.

"No," I responded, stifling a smile. "We are good friends."

Since I have very dark hair, almost black, perhaps she thought I was a member of Mitch's family. When we were all sitting in the visiting yard, I told Mitch about her question, and he just laughed.

The conditions in the visiting yard were still the same as on our first visit. The soda machines were outside in the hall, along with cigarette machines and others for snacks. We learned to stock up on drinks, crackers, vending machine sandwiches, and cigarettes before walking into the visiting yard. That meant we all had soft drinks and snacks to eat during our visit.

The first time we bought Mitch a soda, I remember that he said, "You guys are going to spoil me. I haven't had anything like this in a really long time."

In order to get accustomed to the prison food, and because he had very little money for the first few years, he didn't have luxuries like sodas or most snacks we take for granted. The cigarettes were the only things Mitch could take back to his cell, and the inmates used cigarettes like money in the prison. Mitch didn't smoke, but he could use them to barter with other inmates for better food or other supplies he needed.

Being able to talk face-to-face was a great way to get to know Mitch better and for him to learn about our lives. We often talked on the phone, but that wasn't the same. One conversation in the visiting yard is etched in my memory. Mitch was still on death row, and we were sitting around one of the square tables. Mitch often talked about wanting to get his death sentence reduced to life without parole. After what we had seen of the conditions in prison, I had to ask, "Mitch, if you are executed, you would go to be with the Lord. Doesn't that sound better than spending more years in this prison?"

Mitch was very firm. "No, I want my sentence reduced. I want to get out of prison some day. That's what I am aiming to do."

I thought about this for a moment. "Well, if that is what you want, that's what we will work on."

Mitch asked me a direct question: "Do you think I have a chance of being released?"

I gave him my honest answer. "No, in terms of the laws of Alabama, I don't think you have a chance of that. But with the Lord, things do change, and if you get out, He will get you out. I don't know how that is going to happen, but we will help you when we can."

Mitch nodded and said, "Well, at least you're honest with me. With God's help, we can do it."

One visit was more unusual than the others. We were in

the visiting yard at the table with Mitch, and another death row inmate was at a table across the room with his family members. The entire time we were in the visiting yard, a prison guard sat on a stool between our two tables. I leaned over to Mitch and asked softly, "Why is that guard in here this time?"

"That inmate over there was in one of those white supremacy groups like the KKK," Mitch explained, "and he killed a guy just because he was black. The prison guards think that the black inmates on death row are out to kill him now, but we're not."

It took me a couple of minutes to process all that information.

Adam grew up knowing Mitch and seeing him about once a year during our visits to Holman. When Adam was five or six, Mitch found out that Adam liked to arm wrestle. Mitch would arm wrestle with him on the square table during the visit, and he always let Adam win.

The lack of air-conditioning in the visiting yard was the hardest part. We usually tried to be one of the first families there, to make the most of our time with Mitch. So we were in there by about eight in the morning, and if the visiting yard didn't get too crowded, we could stay until noon or a little later. As more and more families were processed in for their visits, the visiting yard filled and grew hotter and hotter. By noon it was really stuffy and everyone was sweating. The stools around the visiting tables didn't have backs either, and sitting there for hours was pretty tiring, but we were happy to spend time with Mitch and find out more about what was happening to him.

Many rules were enforced during these visits, and some rules even had to do with what the visitors could wear inside the prison. Women weren't supposed to wear sleeveless dresses or blouses. Men and women could not wear shorts. Adam wore shorts when he was small, which was fine. But on one visit, when the three of us reached the building with the visiting yard, the guards told us that Adam was big enough that he also had to wear blue jeans or long pants, no shorts. The guards processed Burt through to the yard while I went back to the car with Adam.

We had just reached our car in the parking lot in front of the prison when I heard Mitch's voice: "Anita! Are they gonna let you in?"

I gave the thumbs-up sign. Obviously Mitch could see us and was worried that we were being turned away. At the same time, I thought about what my mother would say if she knew I was standing there with an inmate in a maximum-security prison calling my name. Adam changed into his blue jeans and we joined Burt in the visiting yard.

Near the end of the visit, when it was stifling hot and almost noon, Mitch said, "It is so nice out here in the visiting yard. I dread going back to my cell."

Burt and I looked at each other. What was difficult to us for four hours was such a treat to Mitch.

LOOK FORWARD TO THE NEXT DAY

by Mitchell Rutledge
Death Row, Holman Prison
March 1, 1986

Today has been like so many days.
All you can look forward to is the next day.
I think you can say I live my life in one day.
Because each day is pretty much the same . . .
See we try so hard to forget just where we are
Which is impossible to do.
We have to also sit back and watch
Our friends, or whatever you want to call them,
Get killed.
Brother Jones is supposed to be killed
  sometime this month
If he don't get a stay, they will kill him.
Now I know this guy.
This guy have been around me and the other
  guys
For 3 or 4 years.
How do you think it feel living beside a guy
  for years
And one day
Someone come to take him somewhere to kill
  him?
That's hard on anyone.

POEM

by Mitchell Rutledge
Death Row, Holman Prison
January 6, 1986

> A guy across the hall
> Started a fire in his cell the other day.
> I don't know why he did it.
> He probably just couldn't take it anymore.
> It be that way sometimes.

PRISON BED

by Mitchell Rutledge
Death Row, Holman Prison
July 22, 1986

> How good it would be
> To go to sleep in a real bed.
> The last 5 ½ years I have been sleeping
> On this prison bed
> Which is 6 feet long and
> 2 ½ feet across.
> I'm not a little person
> And I will tell you
> This bed have got the best of me.

27

SERENGETI PLAINS

Being in prison is like being on the Serengeti Plains.
You have predator and prey. Where would I fit in?

I was still on death row, but I had hope. From that
moment on, I wanted to educate and improve myself. I
wanted to grow emotionally and spiritually because I now
had more to live for. The old Mitch was a loner, a con man
with no real family or friends. I had low self-esteem because
I had no one who believed in an illiterate orphan like me.
The new Mitch had purpose in his life, more focus, and
friends to share life with. Yes, I was still on death row, but
I wasn't alone.

Even life on death row wasn't the same. I felt more confident, and I think my relationships with both guards and

prisoners improved. I had won a certain amount of respect. There are always people trying to tear you down, pronounce you dead, and suck out your hope. But I believed now that God would not let me die there.

I was in the 7-U tier on death row, and that became known as 7-"Unusual." There were fourteen cells on the tier, fourteen guys. If an officer had a problem with one guy, he ended up with a problem with every guy on our tier.

We were creating a special bond among us. We acted as a family, a unit. We shared with one another; if some guy got some money to get something from the store, he shared it. In part this happened because we had a leader— an inmate who was a psychology major in college—who helped us overcome the poisonous atmosphere that prison encourages.

This was unlike my first tier when I came to prison. And I was amazed to have this improvement in prison life, along with my improvement with friends outside the prison. I took it all as a blessing from God. I could see God loved me by the new friends in my life and the improved circumstances in prison. Actually, I became a better inmate because I had focus and something to give. Prison emphasizes taking, but Christianity stresses giving. God gave His only Son, Jesus, and Jesus gave His life for us. My new friends were giving to me, and now I was free to give to others in one of the most hostile environments on earth.

What a test for my new faith.

ANOTHER DAY LESS TIME

by Mitchell Rutledge
Death Row, Holman Prison
June 2, 1986

> *That is what guys say*
> *When they have a date for getting out.*
> *So I would say that saying don't mean*
> *   anything to me.*
> *But I can say*
> *"Each day bring on new hopes."*
> *That is my saying.*

DEATH ROW GAMES

by Mitchell Rutledge
Death Row, Holman Prison
June 4, 1986

> *We did get to stay out for about 3 1/2 hours.*
> *We had something like the death row games.*
> *I couldn't play so I was the official.*
> *The officials get lots of trouble from the*
> *   players.*
> *I got into one argument with a guy*
> *About me making bad calls.*
> *I don't think I was making any bad calls,*

He call me a name and I had to let him know
That I was the official and what I say goes
And there is no need talking more to me
    about it.
Guess what?
The players get two dollars for every game
    they are in.
There are 6 games.
Which mean you can get 12 dollars in all.
The official's supposed to make 5 dollars.
I hope we don't have any trouble trying to get
    our money.

28

NEW FRIENDS

Let me talk about my new friends for a moment. Sister Lillian was like a mother or an older sister for me. She loved me unconditionally—in fact, she was the first person to say "I love you" to me. When she first said that, it had no meaning to me. I had heard people use the word, but it was only a word. I had never felt loved in my life. I told Lillian that, and she replied that she understood but that God had sent her into my life to help me grow as a child of God. That intrigued me. She let me call her on the phone, and the more I got to know her, the more I could see that she was pouring herself into my life.

Lillian had very little money, but she would drive down to Alabama from California during the summer (she taught school during the rest of the year) and stay much of the summer just to see me on visiting days twice a month. She was consistent, and through her actions I saw God's love demonstrated. She believed in me and always urged me to continue learning about life and growing in faith.

Lillian even visited my family and brought my two brothers to prison to see me. When she learned that my grandmother's house had problems with roaches and other pests, she paid for an exterminator to visit the house and spray regularly for a while. To pass the time in my cell, Lillian encouraged me to try to draw or paint, and I did some of that too. I sent several drawings to Lillian as time passed. She also liked getting my poems. She said they gave her a lot of insight into my life and the way I thought about things.

Burt, the college professor, also wrote to me regularly and visited me every year, often with his wife, Anita, and young son, Adam. Burt also let me call them regularly, and he and Anita spoke into my life in a special way. He encouraged my spiritual development, my regular Bible reading, and he believed I could influence people with my mind and my knowledge. He saw me as teachable and a leader of men. He constantly spoke victory into my life. He was the first man (other than my lawyer) to exert a positive influence on me. He was like a big brother to me.

Pam, the Virginia housewife, was and is a special person in her own right. She began writing me after Sister Lillian and the college professor, and she also encouraged my growth with God. I liked her honest approach to our relationship. She explained that if her husband asked her to stop writing, she would have to stop. He was concerned about her writing a prison inmate, and I could understand that. After she told me that, I anticipated that each contact I had with her might be my last. And that saddened me a bit because she, too, believed in me, and I thrived on that. But she kept writing. Her husband, in a way, believed in me, too, by allowing her to continue writing me. I couldn't make phone calls to her or have visits from her, but one day she wrote that she was praying to be able to come and visit me.

Well, time passed and her brother, Bill, began writing me. Pam had told him and her two sisters, Gwen and Rachel, about me, and now they were also in touch. Bill said his sisters spoke highly of me, and he wanted to get to know me. Pam eventually was able to visit me with one of her sisters, and then more of her family members began visiting me regularly. That was really great.

So with the Catholic sister, the college professor and his wife and son, and the Virginia housewife and her family, I had a whole new family of friends and regular chances to improve my letter-writing skills. I had friends who could enjoy my progress and share my errors and my occasional moodiness.

I learned that God is real, that He is present, and that He cares for me. Each new friend helped make me the person I am. God was touching my life daily, and I was growing spiritually and reading better all the time. Whenever I lay down at night deep in a death row prison cell, I could sleep more peacefully because I was no longer alone.

FREEDOM

by Mitchell Rutledge
Death Row, Holman Prison
November 10, 1985

> I have been looking over the word freedom
>   for a while
> And freedom is a thing within.
> As the saying go
> You can put chains around my legs
> But you can't put them around my mind.
> And that is a true saying.
> So when it come down to it
> Freedom is a condition of the mind.
> So it would be true to say I can be as free in
>   this cell
> As anyone living in a 20-room home.
> I feel very free sometimes,
> At other times I feel there will never be a
>   chance
> Of me ever living in the supposed free world,
> Which is something we living in prison all
>   want.

NEW FRIENDS

We live in hope of one day having our
    freedom back
But I think that we can be as free in here
As we could on the outside world.
Now that's not to say that other people in
    prison
Feel the same way.

29

ONE LAST TRY TO ESCAPE EXECUTION

Even though life on death row was a challenge, I was growing and learning in so many ways. I was writing and expressing my feelings in print. Over time Pam introduced me to her mother. Pam had grown up in a navy family, and her parents had retired in northern Florida, which isn't very far from Holman. Pam's father had actually been an admiral in the US Navy, and her mother was a very cultured lady.

So I printed a letter to her mother very carefully. After we had exchanged a few letters, the admiral's wife asked me why I only printed. I said that was all I knew to do, and she sent me an alphabetical list of all the letters in cursive writing. She said she only wanted to receive letters from me in cursive—so I had to learn that. All the letters of the alphabet going in different directions was a challenge, and I spent many hours a day for almost a week trying to master the different strokes. But I was eager to learn as long as people were out there who cared about me learning. I wrote her a letter completely in cursive, and she responded by telling me how proud she was of me for making that advance.

In my unsuccessful sentencing trial in 1985, the district attorney made the statement in his closing argument that as long as Alabama's legislators were in charge, there would be no such thing as life without parole for me. Therefore, the only sure way to keep me off the streets was to give me the death penalty. Well, I knew some guys in prison who were serving life without parole. Three years later, the state of Alabama refuted the district attorney and declared there was life without parole. Dennis, being the good lawyer that he is, sprang into action. He seized upon certain "irregularities" in the last trial, and I was able to get a new sentencing hearing. It was my last chance to leave death row. Dennis was honest with me and said the district attorney would make no mistakes the second time—I would be executed if we lost.

For the new sentencing hearing, I was taken to the county jail in Lee County again, where I was processed by the county authorities. I was not allowed to bring most of my few possessions into the county jail (which is more stringent than the prison on property), and I was put in a soundproof cell and locked inside. I had a small window and I could see a little bit into the jail, but I was very isolated.

Dennis came to visit me to prepare me for the trial, and Sister Lillian was able to come with him. She was startled to see me in chains and said they had the repulsiveness of slavery. I was just pleased to have friends to talk with, and I was excited that the college professor and his wife, Burt and Anita, would both testify for me, along with Lillian, at my final trial.

30

MITCH'S LAST CHANCE

ANITA'S STORY

Several years had passed since we first met Mitch, and Burt and I had more knowledge to use if we testified. Our son, Adam, was three years old. We packed up the car and the three of us drove down to Opelika.

I met Mitch's family—his brothers and his sister, his grandmother and Aunt Dewbell. I also met Lillian for the first time face-to-face. We had corresponded at times during the past six years, and Lillian had even sent Adam a stuffed panda bear with a Christmas ornament attached for his first Christmas back in 1985. We still put that ornament on our Christmas tree each year.

Burt and I met briefly with Dennis and Joni Balske, along with one of Dennis's assistants. The Balskes were a great-looking couple and would impress a jury, I thought. Dennis reminded me of Robert Redford, the actor. I couldn't help tweaking Dennis a bit about his politics. At the time, I was county chairman of the Republican Party where we lived.

"Dennis," I teased, "I just want to make sure that you are aware that two of your star witnesses are arch Republicans."

Dennis got a big laugh out of that. He had already told Burt at the earlier trial that he had never expected two Republicans from Kentucky to become interested in Mitchell Rutledge.

The day of the trial was a long one. Burt had warned me about Mr. Myers, the district attorney, so I was trying to prepare mentally for what was coming. There was a parade of witnesses for the prosecution's side. Yes, Mitch had killed a man; yes, he was a repeat offender; and yes, a jury had already sentenced him to death.

I couldn't be in the courtroom until I testified, and Dennis had scheduled me as the next to last and then Burt as the last witness of the day, so I was hearing about the proceedings secondhand. Also, Adam was with us. During that long day, as the prosecution put on its case, Adam and I read books out in the hall and walked around a bit. We spent a lot of time going up and down in the courthouse elevator. (I know letting your child play in an elevator is not ideal, but try keeping a three-year-old occupied all day in a courthouse.) We didn't get to talk with Mitch at all.

Finally, Dennis began his case for the defense. Mitch's family members testified, and then Lillian made an emotional appeal for a reduced sentence. Finally, my turn as a witness came, and I left Adam and Lillian out in the hall. Lillian had offered to babysit while I was in the courtroom.

I walked into the courtroom and was sworn in as a witness. I took my place on the witness stand and looked around. Mitch looked so nice in the sports coat and tie that Dennis had provided. They were sitting at the defendant's table, of course, and Myers was behind the prosecutor's table. The jury was in place.

Before I answered anything, Dennis and Mr. Myers began arguing in front of the judge's bench about some legal point in my testimony—I can't remember what exactly. The judge asked the jury to step out of the courtroom while he discussed this with the two attorneys and made his ruling. With the jury out of the room, finally the judge said that I could testify.

The judge ordered the jury brought back, and Dennis began asking me questions. I explained how I had become acquainted with Mitch and how my husband and I had visited him in prison several times and corresponded with him regularly. I said that Mitch was sorry for his crime and I believed his repentance was real. He wanted to make a contribution to society, and hopefully the jury would agree to get him off death row.

As I spoke, I was looking at the jury, and one female juror in particular was listening very intently. I thought I was getting through to her, but I couldn't be sure. If one juror refused to give the death penalty this time, the sentence would be reduced.

And then Myers stood up to ask me questions. He had quite a strong personality with witnesses that opposed him—very hostile and often sarcastic. Myers tried to paint Mitch as a "feel sorry for me" liberal who claimed to be one of society's victims of growing up under bad circumstances.

"Mrs. Folsom, do you think that inmates should be released just because they grow up in very bad situations?" Myers asked.

"No," I responded, "and I've never heard Mitch say that either. He regrets his actions. I've never heard him blame his situation."

Myers was convinced that we were working with Mitch because we wanted to publish a book about his life right away for financial gain. He seemed to know that Burt had published several history books and frequently wrote articles for professional journals.

"Are you involved with Mitch to make money writing about it?" he asked.

"No!" I said emphatically.

Burt and I had absolutely no plans to write a book about Mitch's life at that time. And I could have told Myers, if I'd had the opportunity, that anyone who thought our relationship with Mitch was a money-making proposition should examine the facts of the situation.

Finally my time on the witness stand ended. I went out in the hall to check on Lillian and Adam. Burt was on the stand, but I couldn't take Adam in there, so I waited in the hall. Burt said that Myers asked him some of the same questions.

31

THE JURY'S VERDICT

The jury at least got to hear from some people who cared about me and who withstood the district attorney's harsh attacks on me. Dennis was always calm and polite; the district attorney was angry and shrill. I don't blame Myers; he was just doing his job. But it did hurt to hear what a reprobate he thought I was. After the testimony and the concluding statements, the jury went out to deliberate.

When the jury returned, I became nervous. I met the eyes of the first juror who came back into the courtroom; she was a little old white lady and, after locking eyes with me, she looked down and began to cry. Uh-oh. Dennis saw that, too, and began rubbing my back and said, "I'm sorry, Mitch."

The judge then asked for the jury's decision, and the bailiff brought it to him.

The judge read the verdict: "Life without parole."

We had won!

Dennis and Joni were clearly startled, and so were Burt and Anita. Lillian burst into tears. It took a few moments for the good news to sink in. An unusual group of people—black and white, male and female, liberal and conservative—had united to get me, Mitchell Rutledge, off death row, and we had won! The judge announced that in two weeks he would give his decision. He had the final word, and he could still overturn the jury's verdict.

The judge dismissed the jury. Myers was furious, and when Joni walked over to shake his hand, Myers refused. But the judge ordered him to shake her hand, and he did shake it. And then Myers wiped his hand off in front of her.

Those two weeks while I waited for the judge's final verdict were both wonderful, because of the prospect of life that had become real, and agonizing, because the judge could dash my hopes and overrule the jury. The shower in my cell dripped, and I heard a constant dripping during those two weeks. I wrote a poem, "In Prison Within a World, Within a World," during that time.

Finally, I went to hear the judge's verdict. He asked if I had anything to say before he gave his verdict.

"No sir," I said.

As he gave his verdict, he said over and over that he didn't want to give the decision he was about to give. But he was going to give it anyway.

There it was: "Life without parole."

He had accepted the jury's decision. Man had said I would die, but God said, "Live."

IN PRISON WITHIN A WORLD, WITHIN A WORLD

by Mitchell Rutledge
Opelika, Alabama—Lee County Jail
April 18, 1989

As I sit within my world watching life go on,
I see life as it really is.
How? Because time have stood still for me.
As I sit in my window within my world
    watching life,
Life is not unkind nor is it kind.
Life is what man have made of it.
Man have changed life into a game.
What a cruel and ugly game man have
    created.
As I sit and watch it, my heart becomes
    saddened,
My mind confused.
My eyes cry because of what they see.
My ears ache because of the pain they hear.
My voice yells out, "Stop, stop!"
But no one hears me.
My hands reach out to all
But no one cares to take them.

My legs and feet walk the troubled roads
    with you.
But you refuse to acknowledge me.
My body hungers for your love. But no love I
    received.
It could be said it is I,
Who sits and waits within your world.
But within your prison within your world.
Because I were defeated by man's game.
Now I sit and wait, waiting for the game to
    end.
So that each one of us can live
As life was meant to be lived.
For those who comprehend,
Let it be said,
I sit and wait.

32

SEG AND POP

Coming off death row in 1989 was a major victory. My new friends were so happy, and now I would have to show them they put their faith in the right man. After being in an eight-by-five-foot cell for more than eight years, I would now take the step of going into the general population at Holman Prison. Actually there would be three steps from death row to my new life in the general population. First, I spent a month or so in the county jail. Then I was taken down Interstate 65 back to Holman to spend three months in segregation, or "seg" as they called it.

Seg was a transition place for those few who escaped death row and were bound for general population. Seg was also the place for guys who were found guilty of robbing, beating, or raping some person in general population. They were isolated in seg to keep the general population safer. The ironic twist here is that some people also ended up in seg who wanted to be there to escape all the crime and the tough atmosphere in the general population. In seg, you were segregated from others, so there I was again in an eight-by-five cell awaiting my move to general population. I actually knew a few guys in seg, so I wasn't completely isolated.

The physical life in seg may have been the same as in death row, but the atmosphere was different. And oddly that difference was negative, because in seg the prisoners weren't unified. For example, death row had some unity about the place. We were focused; we knew we might be executed at almost any time, and we all shared that prospect. That's why we stuck together on key problems and issues in prison.

But seg was made up of a more scattered group with a variety of people and interests. We had the usual assortment of thieves and killers, but we also had con men and guys who came into prison with light sentences and could have been free if they would have stayed out of trouble. Some of these guys played mind games with you and tried to demoralize or trick you into believing things not true.

After three months of seg, I was finally placed in general population. When I got there, I encountered two homeboys—guys from my neighborhood—from my life on the streets. They were older than I was—one of them had killed some guy on the streets, and the other had, while robbing a gambling house, killed the brother of one of my friends. They knew me and welcomed me to general population, or "pop." There in pop, I had to adjust to a new fast-paced life. On death row and in seg, I was isolated. But in pop, I was with ninety-six other guys in a cell block, and there was always something happening.

It was almost like life back on the streets. I had trouble finding time to get to my new bed and unpack. Even at night, with the lights out, there was always something happening. My first day I kept thinking life would slow down at night and I could sleep soundly, but that wasn't necessarily so. It was dark, so I couldn't read or study, but there was still steady activity—talking, yelling, fighting, raping, and gambling. It was all there. The prison officials, to their credit, strongly opposed much of this, but they didn't have the staff to stop it.

During the first week I was there, I was in the TV room one night watching a program when a guy stumbled through the area bleeding heavily from a knife wound, and then he walked on down the hall. The next night another guy in the living area was severely stabbed at about one in the morning. *Geez*, I thought, *am I back in the Wild West?*

The culture of pop was that guys resolved their differences with knives, and there were no rules for resolving differences. If you wanted to survive, you slept with one eye open. Each day you ultimately had to trust that the guys around you wouldn't kill you that night. Your bed, the kitchen, the TV room, and the living area were all possible arenas for a knife fight.

33

A PRISON MURDER

After surviving my first two weeks in general population—with special praise to God for making me six foot
three, muscular, and able to intimidate people with an ugly
frown—I was allowed to sign up for the prison's GED program, where I could finally get some of the education on the
inside that I never got on the outside. School was from 7:00
a.m. to 3:00 p.m., and I was up for it this time because now
I could read. I just hoped I wasn't too old to learn.

The teacher was white and had trouble connecting with
the primarily black culture in prison. Many prisoners, for
example, were only in class to enjoy some air-conditioning,
which was nonexistent in general pop. Others had learning
disabilities and didn't connect well with the material. Even

though the teacher would teach, few people were learning. He seemed to be just going through the motions sometimes, and so were the students. But I made an effort to connect with him because I wanted to learn.

After I began attending class, he gave me an aptitude test. Yes, I was nervous. On my previous tests, when I was illiterate, I barely scored above moron level, and *Time* shouted that fact to the world. This time I made it onto the scale but not at a high level. I knew little about math, literature, and history. He showed me my scores, and I was on a fourth-grade level here, a third-grade level there, and maybe a fifth-grade level in another area. But the teacher was astonished that I had taught myself to read. He praised my performance and said I had potential. Anyway, I jumped headlong into all the subjects.

If I couldn't understand something or figure it out, I asked the teacher. I was up at his desk often, and he may have tired of me. Some of my peers were tired of my questions too. Their attitude was, "Hey, don't ask him. He don't know nothing. Who cares what he knows?"

Frankly, I cared. I knew about their lives, the street life, and prison, but I wanted to know more about how the outside world worked. Our teacher seemed to know something about that. Sure, he didn't connect well with the class, but he had some knowledge to offer me, and I paid attention.

I discovered that everything that goes on in society also goes on in prison. That includes drugs, drinking, marriage, prostitution, extortion, gambling, loan-sharking, robbery, and especially homosexuality. Much of this activity centers around intimidation. With all this going on in a very limited space, I really had to find my own safe path: reading the Bible for spiritual support, going to school for intellectual support, and working out for physical support. I was going to be different. And I knew I could do it because God had my back.

Before long, I saw my first prison murder. The players in this tragedy were CJ and Runner. Someone stole CJ's tennis shoes, and he assumed Runner was the culprit.

Before going further, I need to explain locker boxes. Each prisoner in population is given a locker box with a combination lock for keeping his possessions. The box is about two feet wide, three feet long, and a foot and a half deep. Prisoners are given a toothbrush and some items made in the prison—thin, poor-quality socks, underwear, and T-shirts. We each get a pair of boots when we first arrive and a roll of toilet paper each week. If we leave any of these items outside our boxes or in the bathroom area, they can and will be stolen—even if we walk away for only fifteen seconds. If we have family members who care about us, they can send us money to buy other items to improve our lives. Tennis shoes are high on this list, and most prisoners want a good pair.

CJ had a good pair of tennis shoes, and he accused Runner of stealing them. CJ confronted Runner and said, "If you do not have my shoes back under my bed at 6:00 p.m., I will kill you."

Who knows whether or not Runner stole the shoes? But he just sat there between their beds, sitting on his locker box with his back to the wall, getting high on dope. He was a tough guy, and he dismissed CJ, who was much weaker. A minute after six that night, Runner learned that CJ was serious. CJ crept up behind Runner with a ten-inch knife and stabbed him clean through his back. Then, even though the first blow was probably fatal, he stabbed Runner twice more for good measure.

CJ backed off, and some of the guys put Runner in a blanket to carry him off. One of the carriers cried out, "He's still alive!" at which point CJ ran up to him, knife in hand, crying, "That swine better be dead!" The guys dropped the blanket, and CJ looked down at a dead man.

One of the guys said, "Don't hit him no more, he is dead already."

CJ responded, "Good!"

Finally, the officers sauntered over and took CJ away—knife in his hand, by the way, as he made his exit. The guards had a tradition of allowing the survivors of knife fights to walk out of the crime scene with their knives. History had shown that if you give up your knife while still in the area of the crime, the partner—or partners—of the person you stabbed would attack you before you could exit the cell block. In this case, Runner lived in Two Block, and he had a partner down the hall in One Block. Later that night, Runner's partner T and CJ's partner GN were put in segregation. The word was that CJ got his knife from his partner GN. The guards didn't want to chance a second fight between T and GN, so both went into segregation.

The only way out of segregation is for both parties to sign a prison form called the "peace treaty," which says you agree to live with your adversary in peace. Having signed the peace treaty, if you are killed, your family cannot sue the prison system later. In this case, after twenty-seven days, T and GN both signed the peace treaty and went back to general population. The next morning, while GN was sitting in the Law Library looking over legal work, T, in retaliation, crept up behind GN and stabbed him to death in the back—the same way CJ had killed T's partner Runner.

A week later, two or three guys stabbed another partner of Runner and T, and they also beat him with a baseball bat. A few days later, GN's nephew, in his bed sleeping, was stabbed in the eye and blinded, but he did fight back and was able to save his life (but not his eye). The warden began transferring guys on both sides of the dispute out of the camp. That ended the feud.

34

THREE PRISON VICES

Since I was new to prison and wanted to survive, I decided to look up one of my homeboys for advice. I asked him about getting a knife—a good knife would cost about fifteen to twenty dollars, and a long knife with a handle and guard would run about fifty dollars. Some prisoners specialized in knife making: they usually took the hinge off of a locker box and sharpened that long hinge on the floor into a point. Some prisoners also made ice picks out of any steel object that had a point grinded onto it. My homeboy gave me good advice. He said, "Mitch, you may not need a knife if you stay away from gambling, getting in debt, and the gay lifestyle." He was right—those three areas caused the most resentment and violence.

A larger issue is intimidation and how you carry yourself in prison. Are you perceived as weak, in which case predators will come for you, or strong, in which case you may be left alone? One of my homeboys, Dusty, helped show me this distinction. Dusty was a tough guy and he respected me as a strong person. One day he introduced me to Big Grind, who had a reputation as a "dog." That's prison slang for a guy who cares for no one and plays by his own rules.

Big Grind was in great physical shape and had a reputation as a killer—not that he necessarily had killed anyone, but he was seen as someone who might. One day when Dusty and I were talking, Big Grind walked by. Dusty and Big Grind respected each other, and Dusty said, "Big Grind, this is my little homeboy, or I should say big homeboy."

When you are being introduced to a predator, you must carry the conversation from start to finish with eye-to-eye contact. Without moving. We both did that, and Big Grind said, "Mitch, you are going to hear a lot of things about me—most of it not good. Most people don't like me because I step on the weak. If I don't, someone else will. If you are strong, you have no problem out of me unless you get in my path."

He lived that just as he spoke it. He lived in Three Block, and he had three or four partners who would have gone to war with him. He also had about ten to fifteen "boys," which in the Alabama prison system means homosexuals. Big Grind pimped them out. He would also sell one or two if the price was right. A young guy might get $200 or $300 on the prison market.

Most people in prison are caught up in homosexuality. They arrive with no intention of going in that direction, but they get trapped. When a person arrives in prison, he usually has little money and few friends. A predator will trap a new guy by pretending to befriend him. First comes an offer of coffee, cigarettes, or maybe some pot. A promise of protection may come next. The new guy becomes dependent on the predator and owes him money. Since he depends on the predator, the new guy is, in the eyes of prisoners, like a woman or girlfriend to him.

The new guy is drawn into homosexuality as a repayment and as a means of preserving his protection. If the predator is into homosexuality, the new guy becomes his personal boy, but the predator often sells his boys to the highest bidder. Those with little homosexual experience get a higher bid than those who have been passed around. I've known guys to be sold for only two bags of coffee, or about four dollars.

Big Grind and I never had a problem. I didn't agree with what he was doing, but I never confronted him or gossiped about him. We respected each other, and respect is what is needed to survive in prison.

Gambling is another major vice of prison life. Sometimes inmates would have running poker games that would go two to three days. The guys running the game would get a house cut, and they would take multiple-hour shifts running the game for the players, who would come and go. Other guys with sandwiches, weed, and wine would come by selling their stuff, and those who were winning could afford to treat themselves. Sometimes the losers would get a credit extension, but they were slaves or dead men if they didn't pay back with interest. Sometimes losers would try to rob another player or the guy running the game. Weaker guys had to be careful among the stronger players or a fight would result. I avoided all this and focused on positive things.

I had to read the Bible to keep up my hope and to think along positive lines in such a negative environment. I also had to stay strong and I asked a homeboy, Big Loose, if he would be my partner and work out with me in the weight yard. He agreed. I knew Big Loose from the streets of Columbus, Georgia. Before prison, he had owned a few Cadillacs and had many runners under him who were able to run dope and prostitution because of his protection.

My workouts with Big Loose and his friend Big Ben stretched me. They were both in great shape from weight training, and I had trouble keeping up with them the first day. When I wanted to rest, Big Ben laughed and said, "Get up, big man, we are just starting." He added, "Big Loose, I thought you said your homeboy wanted to really work out."

Actually, that wisecrack helped break the ice, and I did learn to keep up with them, which put me in great physical condition. I needed to be in good physical as well as spiritual shape to face the challenges of prison. After eight years, I had gone from a small single cell on death row to a cell block with ninety-six guys. It was like being back on the streets with all the dangers and con games.

I told God, "Hey, You saved me for a reason, and that reason is not to get dragged down by street life or prison life." As much as possible, I stayed out of trouble by working out, reading my Bible, and writing to and thinking about my friends on the outside. That gave me hope instead of the hell inside the prison. No, I was not perfect, and once or twice I did some weed and bought some prison wine. After doing that, I felt embarrassed and asked God for forgiveness.

I confessed my failings to Sister Lillian and Professor Burt and his wife, Anita, and they stood strong behind me. If God would give me friends on the outside and protection on the inside, I believed I could stay strong and pass the test of prison life. I pursued my GED degree and studied hard.

I resisted the gay lifestyle in prison. Many guys who knew me gave me credit for this by saying, "Man, you are strong," but I would stop them and say, "It is not me, it is God. If it were not for Him, I would most likely have me a boy."

They would just smile, and we would continue the conversation in another direction.

I never considered myself better than those who failed in prison. I never looked down on them. I just had a higher force that they didn't. Without a relationship with God, the prison life will pull you under—especially if you have life without parole, which is called "the living death sentence."

THE DEN OF JACKALS

by Mitchell Rutledge
Holman Prison
February 1, 1996

I'm living in the den of jackals.
The jackals I'm speaking of
Are ones that walk upright.
Every jackal performs dishonest and base
 deeds
For his own or another's gain.
It's a hard fight living this life
With the jackals.
Every jackal is trying to step on the other
 one,
Or use the other one.
It's a game in the den of jackals.
The only rule is: no rule.
Introducing young and innocent prey
To the laws of the game
That mistreat everything and everyone
Creates a monster.
Innocence and fairness is only a joke
In the den of jackals.
The only things they respect
Are lies, envy, jealousy, hate.
All of these things are welcome

THREE PRISON VICES

And a delightful topic at any campfire
In the den of jackals.
Life is only given to the strongest jackals.
The weakest ones become prey.
It's the beast from within that rules
In the den of jackals.

35

GED

One positive focus I had was getting my GED, or General Educational Development, which is the equivalent of a high school degree. I wanted the education I never got in school. In *Up from Slavery*, Booker T. Washington says, "From the time that I can remember having any thoughts about anything, I recall that I had an intense longing to learn to read."[1]

He learned to read, and so did I. Washington said he was determined that "if I accomplished nothing else in life, I would in some way get enough education to enable me to read common books and newspapers."[2] Education was Washington's way out of slavery and it would be mine too.

Reading and writing were my connections with the

outside world and my freedom in the midst of the slavery of prison. After about one year and nine months, I passed my pre-GED test, and that qualified me to study and take the regular test. When I took the test, I had to wait four to six weeks for the results. All of us who took the test were excited when the teacher called each of us in and said either, "Congratulations" or "Better luck next time."

I was the last man in line, and I heard the teacher say, "Sorry, Mitch, better luck next time." After walking away, I opened my envelope and saw my score. To pass, we needed a score of 45, and I had a 42.6. Yes, I had failed, but I was close. I determined to study harder, and I visualized myself walking through that line with a passing grade.

My two areas of weakness were math and English. So I went around my block asking who knew anyone good in these areas. The name I began hearing was Joe C., who was in my cell block. After lockdown, when lights went out that night, I found Joe C. and asked if he would help me. Joe was a bank robber from the Windy City of Chicago and had a strong midwestern accent. He said, "Yes, I'll be glad to help you."

He had come to Alabama to visit a friend but robbed a bank instead and during the robbery had killed a policeman. Joe was captured and ultimately got life without parole, so he was in the same position I was. God must have led me to him, because he worked with me for hours at a time, helping me to improve my math and my English.

When test time came around again, I was so excited I

drank a full cup of black coffee. Ten of us were present, and I focused on the test and tried to use my time wisely. I put all I had into the math and English questions. Would my studying pay off?

After about five weeks, the GED results came in, and I again got in the very back of the line to wait my turn. Some of the test takers had smiles on their faces, others had frowns—which concerned me because I thought one or two of them were fairly smart. Finally my turn came. The teacher shook my hand, as he did before, but this time he said, "Congratulations, Mitch."

I did it! The man who came to prison as an illiterate had his high school equivalency.

That night I used what money I had to cook a big meal for Joe C. and me. For the main course, I cooked sausage by putting it in a Coke can and using shoelaces to hold it over a fire that we made with lots of toilet paper. We also had soup, cooked the same way. From the prison store, I bought two Cokes, corn chips, cheese curls, and a honey bun. That's about the best meal either of us ever had in prison.

The next morning I looked into signing up for the local college program that was available at Holman. After filling out the forms, I went to the weight yard with Big Loose and Big Ben, and I was bursting with confidence in life.

36

MIND GAMES

As usual, when you get strong on hope in Holman, an obstacle is just around the corner. A week after my GED triumph, one of Big Grind's partners, OT, bumped right into me on the narrow walkway in my cell block. The walkway was only three feet wide, so all of us had to be careful in such cramped space. Emotions and egos were present, and by custom if you accidently bumped another prisoner, you showed courtesy by a quick apology or brief acknowledgment of some kind.

OT bumped me and showed no regret whatsoever. The problem here is one of respect. If you don't maintain respect by constant vigilance, you are perceived as weak, and when that happens your life begins to disintegrate. I wondered if OT, who was a partner of Big Grind's and a strong guy, knocked me on purpose. Since I was cool with Big Grind, I should be cool with OT. So I let it go.

Not long after this, OT and I were crossing each other again, and OT bumped me again and never looked back or said a thing. I was being tested. Would I pass the respect test as well as my GED test? I showed no emotion and said nothing to anybody. But I thought about it. If that had happened on the streets of Columbus before I knew God, I would have retaliated the first time with fists and with weapons if necessary. One of us would have walked away with a brutal beating.

I knew now that God wants us to be strong, but He wants us to be wise and to seek peace when possible. The next time I crossed paths with OT, he bumped me again, and I bumped back much harder. He lost his balance, and before he could recover I was staring right into his face. Looking him in the eyes, I said, "What do you want to do about it, pig?"

He saw no fear, and I had no fear. But I had started no fight yet either. OT said, "My bad," and that ended the confrontation.

OT was a very capable fighter, but I had stopped short of disrespecting him, and he decided a truce was in his best interest. After that, when we crossed each other's path we spoke in a friendly way and that ended the problem.

Shortly afterward, I became cool with a small, smooth guy named Shorty Red. He said one day that reading people was important in prison and that misreading someone could get you hurt real quickly. I was agreeing with him when he startled me by saying, "Mitch, we were going to break into your locker box."

Our locker boxes, as I have said, hold all our possessions. Breaking into someone else's locker box is like breaking into his house. It could start a war. So I said, "What?"

"Yes, we were going to get you."

"Shorty, you were going to do that?"

"Yes," he said. "But we are glad we did not do it because as time went on, we saw that you are a good dude. You are not weak."

I was still unsettled over this and asked, "What made you all want to break into my box?"

He said, "Mitch, when you came down to population, we thought you were just a big, weak dude because you were friendly to everyone. You were giving guys things when they asked you, and even sometimes to people you hardly knew who weren't asking. We thought you were afraid and were trying to buy your way through. We know now that you are just a real good dude."

I marveled at how God was protecting me and even opening doors for me to show in a limited way the love of Christ in this place of despair.

COLD AIR

by Mitchell Rutledge
Holman Prison
February 5, 1996

I'm in the cold corner
In the madhouse they call prison.
There is no insulation,
Only concrete and steel.
At times there is a little heat.
Once that cold set into that steel and
    concrete
Boy is it cold.
My bed is against the wall.
A steel door is about four-and-a-half feet
    away
From the foot of my bed.
Cold air shoots through it.
When it rain,
Water wet everything.
It's very hard to sit up at your bed to write or
    anything.
It's no place to be.
You wouldn't want your pets
To live under these conditions.

37

PRISON CULTURE

In general population at Holman, I learned to try to be a force for peace in an atmosphere of war. I wasn't judgmental. I would talk casually with pimps, whores, murderers, robbers, predators, and prey alike. God opened doors for me to deal with all kinds of people, and I took people and prison life as I found it and tried to make things more livable and more open to God. I didn't form friendships with the inmates. My friends were Lillian, Burt, Anita, and Pam and her family—the people on the outside. They gave me what I needed emotionally.

But in prison I didn't make "friends" because if you make a friend, you can lose your freedom—you have to back the friend in any fights or conflicts he gets into. And if he knows you are his "friend," he might be more likely to pick fights, knowing you will be obligated to rescue him. Thus, I tried to have many good acquaintances, but no friends.

Let me give an example. I began to hang out some with Q and his partner TB. Q was a little guy, and TB was one of the strongest guys in prison. He could press almost five hundred pounds of weight, and few people messed with him. Q and TB sold drugs and were into the gay life. But Q would sometimes look to me for advice, and I tried to help him.

Q and TB began selling drugs for J.Pa., who prospered through a large drug-selling operation. J.Pa. liked to pursue the gay life with young white guys, and he began trapping a young white guy with free drugs. After some free samples, one day Q, TB, and J.Pa. went to collect: either pay with cash or with sex. The guy must have heard what was about to happen, because when Q, TB, and J.Pa. went to his cell block to put on the pressure, he had four friends with knives nearby. When he was threatened, his friends emerged and attacked the three drug dealers. Q took two guys on but was stabbed in the side and through the hand. TB knocked down his two attackers just in time to save J.Pa., who was down and about to be stabbed in the neck. Finally, some officers broke up the fight and threw them all into segregation.

When Q was released back into population, he came to me for some cash and some advice. I had both for him. I asked, "How long are you going to play prison games with your life about things that don't really matter?"

He smiled at me and said, "You are right, Big Brother. I'm going to slow down."

We talked some more, and he left in a calmer state. A week later, TB, J.Pa., and some of the other guys got released after they signed the prison peace agreement.

After a few months, a young mulatto guy named Tap came to population. Lots of people liked him and wanted him for gay sex. Tap said he wasn't into gay sex, but Q began to hang out with him and tried to lure him into the gay life. When Tap said no, Q said, "If you don't want sex, we won't force it on you. But if you ever decide to be part of that life, promise you will be with me."

Tap agreed, and they continued to hang out. Tap showed bravery by jumping a guy who tried to attack Q from behind. Guys said Tap had heart, that he could be a warrior. I even commended him for helping my little brother Q, and Tap said, "Yeah, he is my partner."

But then a Spanish gay guy, whom we will call Carlos, came into population. He seemed to have some money because he had an active sex life. His eyes were especially on Tap, and somehow he secretly lured Tap into the gay life. When Q found out what was going on, he was furious with Tap and Carlos. Q was insane with jealousy, and when I talked with him he kept saying that Tap had promised himself to him, but now was with Carlos. I listened and said forcefully, "Leave that alone. Carlos and Tap don't want you to be part of their thing. And most of the camp is on their side because Tap saved you—he doesn't owe you anything."

Q wouldn't listen; he said Tap had to be his. Carlos did his best to calm things down. In fact, he "bought" Tap from Q for three cartons of Kools. Carlos and Tap didn't have to do that, but they did it with the hope of making peace.

Q, however, wanted more. One day when I had finished jogging on the Big Yard, I saw Q in a heated argument with Carlos and Tap. I called for Q and when I did, Carlos and Tap walked away. Q blurted out to me, "I'm not through with them yet!"

I retorted, "Q, you are wrong. They paid you off well, and you are headed for trouble. Let it go. Have you lost your mind?"

As we continued talking, Q calmed down and said, "Okay, I'm through with it."

I wonder if Q meant it. I will never know because that night at 11:50, Carlos and Tap killed Q. They tricked him by coming to him and offering to give him a back massage. During the massage they pinned him down and stabbed him in the neck. Q tried to fight back, and they stabbed him again. Q's last words were, "Don't let these greaseballs kill me like this. Get them off me so I can fight them!"

No one came to Q's rescue. The prison sense of justice was that he had been paid off and was out of line to keep complaining.

38

COLLEGE

I refused to be sucked under by prison life. I had my GED, and next I took the big step of enrolling in the local college program offered at Holman. I was going to be a college student. I would continue making something of my life. When I was in class, I would do the reading and pay close attention. Many guys took these courses to get a break from population; they paid no attention and just enjoyed the peace and the air-conditioning. As for me, I asked questions and tried to probe the teacher's mind and learn what I could.

Other prisoners put me down for taking these courses so seriously, but no one challenged me to my face. I took courses in English and in history, and I began to thrive in both. Lillian, Burt, Anita, and Pam gave me strong encouragement, and in the next three or so years, I eagerly completed eighty-three hours of college credit, just thirteen credits short of my degree.

My outside friends always asked about my classes and boosted my confidence. They wanted constant progress reports. Burt regularly talked history to me and helped spark my desire to learn more about our country. Pam helped me in several ways. She said that I had shown the ability to learn and improve, even when the classes were difficult. Pam's brother and sisters also came to visit me. The whole family! They knew a lot about how the world worked and had traveled a lot because their father was an officer in the navy. Their brother, Bill, had also become a navy officer. He came to visit several times, and we became friends. I still keep in touch with him and his children. His children, who are grown now, talk with me on the phone and sometimes ask for advice.

Lillian was always so positive and supportive. She sent me a pronunciation guide to help me sound out new words and a table with words broken into syllables. I had a dictionary and wanted to expand my vocabulary, but this was hard because English has many silent letters and exceptions to rules. Also I have a deep Southern accent—I sound a bit like Morgan Freeman in *Driving Miss Daisy*. That movie was set in Atlanta and I grew up in black culture not far to the south and west of Atlanta. Sometimes I would sit on my bed for hours, working on spelling, vocabulary, and pronunciation. It was an honor and a dream to be in college, and I was determined to be a good student.

When I would be sitting there reading and pronouncing new words, sometimes chaos was all around me—fights, gambling, yelling, and so on. But if I could ignore it, I would stick to my studies and continue my work. Inmates noticed this and saw me as different, and that sometimes attracted them to me in a positive way. Sure, some guys said I was wasting my time trying to pass a course when I had life without parole. So what? How would those classes help? But others said, "Hey, you are doing something positive with your life."

After taking new courses semester after semester, I had eighty-three of the ninety-six hours needed for a degree at Jefferson Davis Community College in Atmore. Then came the word that the college program was to be shut down. I was shocked and very disappointed, but I could understand. The program cost the taxpayers money, and some people were saying, "Hey, we have to pay for our own kids' college. Why should we pay for some murderers in prison to go to college at our expense?"

That is a consideration, but college offered hope that we might better ourselves, and in doing so, those of us who would be released could better support ourselves and not be a burden to society again through crime or welfare.

I was sad that I couldn't go from illiterate to college grad in prison, but my outside friends cheered me up. Lillian and Burt both said my education wasn't over. They talked about how proud they were of me and how far I had come.

RACHEL'S STORY

I'm Pam's younger sister, and I lived far from southern Alabama, so by the time I came to know Mitch he was already off of death row. I was fascinated that my mother, an admiral's wife and every inch the proper lady, had become such good friends with Mitch. She would often say, "Who would have thought I'd have a convicted black murderer whom I consider as part of the family?"

My mother insisted that Mitch use good grammar when he wrote letters to her, so I know he worked on grammar and spelling to please her. I finally visited Mitch with my sisters, my brother, and my husband, Joe, who is a navy pilot. We were impressed that at every visit Mitch presented such a good appearance. He obviously made sure his clothes were spotless and his hair was cut. We brought quarters to use in the vending machines, and at the end of visits, Mitch would have packs of cigarettes to take to his cell for bartering with other prisoners.

During one morning on the visiting yard, Mitch explained to Joe and me that he had accumulated a debt with another prisoner. We knew this was a serious thing in prison. Mitch pointed out that the other prisoner was also on the visiting yard that day. We couldn't give the prisoner any money, but we could pay off the debt by giving the prisoner's relatives the money when they left the prison. Would we do that? Mitch asked.

Yes, we agreed to pay off the small debt that Mitch

owed. When the visiting time was over for all the inmates, we left the prison at the same time as the other families. Out in the parking lot, Joe explained to the people Mitch had pointed out that another inmate owed their family member some money, and he was paying the debt off now. As Joe gave them the money, right under the eyes of the guards in the tower, he had the uncomfortable feeling that this transaction looked like a drug deal going down. But he did it anyway, and the family notified their man that the debt was paid.

Mitch said, "There is honor among thieves."

One thing that is very important to Mitch is that you only do things for him out of love and friendship. He doesn't want it to be charity.

And he became part of our family.

BILL'S STORY

I also came to know Mitchell Rutledge through my sister Pam. I was a navy pilot, so I traveled a great deal with my career, but at times my sisters and I would meet at my parents' home in Pensacola for a reunion.

The first time I saw the prison was because Pam and our sister Gwen had scheduled a visit with Mitch, so I drove them over there. Eventually all of us visited Mitch together. I probably visited Mitch six or seven times.

He would call and write letters. My two children grew

up knowing Mitch, and he encouraged them and prayed for them. They asked for his advice more than once. One of Mitch's biggest fears is that people will desert him. He experienced abandonment so many times growing up that he sometimes worries that his friends won't stick with him.

I visited Mitch several times before the prison changed the rules about non-family members visiting inmates. When the rules changed, suddenly I couldn't visit Mitch face-to-face, but we talked on the phone regularly. Also, my wife was diagnosed with Alzheimer's and I have been her caregiver, which takes all my time. Mitch has been praying for me during this time. I'm an elder at my church, and I often read Mitch's letters to our congregation. Mitch's faith is a strong testimony to many people who will never meet him in person but are inspired by the faith of a prisoner serving life without parole.

39

SICKNESS

My next big obstacle came not from my fellow inmates but from the prison staff. Some of the guards and staff show prisoners respect, others show fear, and still others show contempt. Unfortunately, I encountered a prison doctor who treated my life as having no value. It was in 1998.

I had been working out and was buff—two hours with weights each day and running five miles every other day. But I began suddenly to tire more quickly and I lost my appetite. I requested a medical visit, and the doctor took some X-rays and told me I just had the flu. I kept expecting to recover and was annoyed that I still felt so tired and weak. I couldn't do my regular workouts, and I seemed to lose more strength every day.

One day a female officer called me through a narrow opening in a prison window. "Mitch, are you okay?" she asked. And before I could respond, she added, "You don't have AIDS, do you?"

I said I don't go that route and I thought she knew that.

She said, "I heard you didn't, and I've never seen you go in that direction, but I thought that about other guys, too, and I was wrong. But what's your problem?"

I said, "The flu."

"Mitch," she said, "the biggest thing on your body is your head. You look bad."

When I talked with Sister Lillian about this, she insisted I go to the doctor for another checkup. I did that, and he again said I had the flu. When I told Lillian, she accepted it and said, "I don't believe a doctor would lie to you about a serious medical condition." Well, I gradually got worse, and it got to the point that I could only sit on the edge of my bed with my head in my hands. I could hardly move beyond that. While this was happening, I was surprised at how many guys came by to wish me well. One said, "I hear you are dying," which hardly cheered me up, but at least he cared and had said it with regret.

God helped in the form of a nurse. A hospital runner came by and said I was wanted at the pick-up window. When I got there, I met a nurse who had become interested in my case. "Do you have family who cares about you?" she asked.

I said no, but I have friends outside who care.

She said, "You are really sick."

I said, "Yeah, I have the flu."

"No," she said, and what came next stunned me: "The doctor is lying to you."

"Really?" I said. "What's wrong with me?"

"I can't tell you that, but you are real sick and the doctor is lying. You had better let your friends know."

I called Sister Lillian, who had moved to Alabama to be near me, and she called the prison commissioner the next day.

Two days later, I was called into the infirmary, and the head nurse told me to go in and sit down. The doctor, however, refused to see me. The head nurse told him, "You have no other choice. You have been ordered to tell him what is in his medical files."

Finally, the doctor came in and told me that the x-rays I had taken months ago showed two large lymph nodes in my lungs, which indicated either tuberculosis or cancer. I looked at the doctor and said, "You were going to let me die."

He responded, "It doesn't make sense to spend money on a man who has life without parole." Those were his amazing words. Later, I discovered he had lied about serious medical conditions to five or six other guys who were serving life without parole.

With my condition now exposed, I was taken to the hospital to see various specialists. It had been ten years—my last court hearing—since I had been outside the prison.

I was in chains and under heavy guard, but I looked at cars, people, trees, and the parking lot. It was all so unfamiliar. When an officer asked what I thought of the free world, I said, "It's beautiful."

I was taken to the hospital in a white prison van marked "Alabama Prison" all over it. When we stopped, the officer left me chained in the van while he went in the hospital to deal with admissions. Many curious onlookers stared at the van. When I was taken out of the van, I was chained down, and some people walking by looked at me as though I were a wild animal. Some looked at me with fear, and others looked so sad.

In the hospital, I was told to sit. Soon a young nurse came in. She also looked uncomfortable, so I smiled at her. That settled her a bit, and she asked me some basic questions. When finished, she asked how long I had been in prison. "Eighteen years," I said, and she stepped back and looked as if to say, *What did you do to get that sentence?* Instead, she asked how much more time I had left. "By man's law I have been condemned for life," I said, but I said to myself, *But not according to God.*

When the nurse left, a lung specialist came in. He smiled and said, "Good afternoon, Mr. Rutledge. I'm Doctor Thomas. I want you to know I'm not concerned about what you are in prison for. To me you are just another patient."

My X-rays from the prison doctor hadn't arrived yet, so that limited his ability to compare changes in my tumors, but he took new X-rays.

When they took me to the X-ray room, the people in the hospital gawked at me, wondering what such a dangerous person, chained, was doing in there. Little did they know how weak I felt. I couldn't have terrorized a fly. I was just glad to have my x-rays taken. I sat down, head in my hands, and prayed hard for the Lord to guide the diagnosis.

Meanwhile, the prison X-rays arrived. Dr. Thomas came in my room and said, "Mr. Rutledge, I have good news and bad news. Which one do you want to hear first?"

"The good news," I said, because there had been nothing but bad so far.

He showed me two pictures. "Here are the lymph nodes. Can you see them?" I was too weak to stand up and look at them, so he brought them over to me. "Notice that the lymph node in the more recent X-ray is smaller. That would never happen if the tumor were cancer. You don't have cancer. The bad news is that you have tuberculosis."

With that news, I was wheeled away. I stayed the night in the hospital, chained to a bed on the ninth floor, and then I was moved to one prison and then another. I was kept in isolation and had to wear a mask whenever I left the cell. And they notified Sister Lillian, who had been recently exposed to me. I received treatment from another helpful doctor who said, "If we had not taken action, another two or three months might have been too late."

With active TB, the prison staff avoided me and I was kept in isolation for thirty days. But they did say I could contact family. Of course, I only had the family God had given me, and when I told them what had happened, they sprang into action. My prison cell was soon full of sandwiches and ice cream I had bought with money sent from Lillian, Burt and Anita, and Pam. I began to eat again and gained some weight. I did a lot of praying during those thirty days. I prayed for complete recovery—God had preserved me this far. My life had purpose, and I wanted to continue to live and to make a difference in the world. Even from my cell.

After thirty days, the prison said I could leave isolation. I was taking medication, and the tuberculosis was in remission. Because this prison wanted to put me in segregation—for dangerous prisoners—not population, I appealed to be returned to Holman, where I would take the medication and be returned to the general population.

Instead, I was taken to Kilby Prison in Montgomery, where prisoners are sometimes processed before going to other prisons in the state. Because of the tuberculosis, they put me in segregation—no contact with other prisoners except for a daily forty-five-minute walk in leg irons. One of the guys there heard the news that a Mitchell Rutledge from Holman had arrived. He said, "The only Mitchell Rutledge from Holman who I know died a couple of months ago." His name was Chi, and I knew him from Holman.

When I saw Chi on my daily walk, he was amazed to see me because he had heard that I died. On the walk, I was in pain because the chains and leg irons fit so poorly that they were scraping the skin off my ankles. "Mitch," Chi said in greeting, "you are supposed to be dead."

I responded, "I feel like I am. These leg irons are killing me."

Chi smiled, and other guys who knew me were saying hello and treating me with respect. This astonished the officers, who wondered, *Who is this new guy who is commanding such attention and respect?*

I mention this because that respect I received was a pleasant moment in a nightmare of phony diagnoses, physical weariness, X-ray concerns, gawking strangers, and misplacement in segregation with chains and leg irons. To the Holman doctor, and many others, I was a discard, a wasted and meaningless life. But those prisoners who knew me were calling out to me with recognition and admiration. That forced the guards to take me seriously, and all of that would eventually help get me transferred back into population and back to Holman.

Let me make something clear. The respect from other prisoners that startled the guards was not because I was big and bad, or because I was a warrior or killer. That respect was accumulated over time because I was a man of my word, because I didn't play mind games, sex games, and domination games, and because I treated everyone—weak or strong— with respect. I was not better than the other prisoners, but I had something most of them didn't have: God. His grace and His love kept me strong in the midst of chaos. I could reach out to others because I had His strength at my back.

Almost twenty years after the *Time* article, which said I was "defective" and urged readers to forget about me, that first prison doctor also said I was a throwaway. But God believed my life had value, and He had given me a purpose. I believed that my best was yet to come.

40

SORRY, CHARLIE

After four more months of recovery, I was on the train for a two-hour ride back to Holman. On the train with me were some new convicts on the way to Holman for the first time. I sat next to Charles, who had life without parole and had never been to Holman but had heard how rough it was. Holman gets those who are too violent for other prisons.

Charles knew that, and he asked me all types of questions. He was scared, as all incoming prisoners are, but he was doing his best not to show it. I explained the rules at Holman, formal and informal, and tried to help him get ready to enter prison. On the train, he could see I had people who respected me, so he said, "I see you have some friends."

I said, "No, I know a lot of people because I've been in here eighteen years. Having 'associates' and having 'friends' are two different things. So-called friends will sometimes play games with you to get something out of you, and you had better learn that real fast. Every day people are going to play mind games with you. Avoid the wrong crowd. I will introduce you to some guys who might be helpful to you." I wanted Charles to succeed, and I gave him my word that I would help him.

When we got to Holman, I told Charles what he could expect. But what I didn't expect was the outpouring of interest, and even affection, for my return. The officers immediately greeted me with, "We heard you had died," to which I responded, "Are you disappointed?" We all laughed and I was glad to be back.

After I was processed, the prisoners greeted me with smiles and affection. "Man, we heard you had died," they said again and again. Well, they said that about Lazarus, too, but the Lord delivered both of us. Anyway, I made it to my bed and had a good sleep, but when I woke up, more prisoners came to me wanting to talk and learn more about what I had been through.

In all the excitement, I lost track of Charles. I knew how nervous I had been when I came to Holman, and I wanted to check up on him. I found him and said, "Hey, I didn't mean to overlook you, man. How are you doing?"

He said, "Gee, you have a lot of friends," and that worried me right off because he wasn't yet seeing the difference between "friends" and "associates." I took Charles around and introduced him just to guys I thought might be okay for him.

After that, I went to Gibb, one of my homeboys who had a store, and I told him to let Charles have a little bit and put it on my account. Gibb said that since the food was for the new guy, he would have to put the normal interest rate of 25 percent on it. Later I introduced Charles to Gibb, and afterward I told Gibb to help me look out for him.

About a month later, Gibb pulled me aside and said, "Homeboy, this guy you introduced to me, he is traveling in circles that are not good for him."

I said, "Okay," and later pulled Charles aside. "My homeboy tells me you are traveling in dangerous circles. These guys you are dealing with will turn on you and bring sex games to you if they see any weakness in you. You need to know that."

Charles shrugged it off. "I'm not worried about that. We are cool."

I said, "Okay, well, I've warned you," and he walked off. I could see Charles was not strong enough to travel with these guys and stay clean.

About one month later, I happened to see Charles's "friends" "talking" to him under his clothes. Charles was treating it like a joke, nothing serious. But it was the slow beginning of sexual advances. Then Charles's "friends" were buying him pot and booze. These presents were subtly obligating him to them, but he didn't see it.

Six months later, Charles came to me, frantic.

"These guys are putting pressure on me to have sex with them," he said.

"I explained what would happen if you continued to travel with them. What do you expect me to do?"

"Talk with them."

"What can I say?"

"Let them know I'm not like that."

"It doesn't make any difference what anybody says at this point," I said. "They are not going to let up on you because they want you, and you now owe them. You have played their game and either you will have sex with them or they will stab you, or you will stab them. If you stab them, that will get you into segregation and that will protect you but at the cost of permanently isolating you."

Not long after this, word was out that Charles began having sex with them. From that point, he went on to do every imaginable sexual perversion.

Charles is one of many who failed, but at least I tried to help.

41

HONOR DORM

Life in the general population is better than isolation in seg, but living with so many troubled people was a constant challenge. Prison reformers, led by Chuck Colson, came up with the idea of an Honor Dorm, designed for those inmates who could be rehabilitated. They would live as a community. They would be given tasks and held accountable for completing those tasks. When Holman announced the forming of an Honor Dorm, I was interested in improving myself and in working with the more serious inmates. When I asked Lillian and Burt and Anita about the Honor Dorm, they were enthusiastic and told me to go for it. Lillian made the point that if I did well in the Honor Dorm, that might improve my chances for eventual release.

I filled out the application form and was accepted. In fact, the chaplain called me in and asked if I would take a leadership role—head up one of the major programs. I was flattered to be asked, and I liked the Honor Dorm concept, but the more I learned about how it would work, the more concerns I had. I guess my ideal Honor Dorm would be a world where inmates could work to earn money (in part to pay restitution to those they hurt) or work to improve their education or their skills for life after prison. With that I think you would see prisoners eager to be there and pursue real rehabilitation.

Our Honor Dorm was a step forward, but not quite along the lines I hoped for. I was asked to head the audio-visual department and be accountable for proper use of the two televisions. In other words, I was to be more of a bureaucrat and enforcer. The television is a big deal in prison because it is a rare form of legitimate entertainment behind bars. You can escape from prison life in the evening and learn some about what's happening outside through television. Whoever controls the television does indeed have power, but he also has to make and enforce rules—and that may make him some enemies. I preferred to lead by example and then talk with prisoners who were interested in what they saw in me. Instead, I would have to supervise the television, a major source of interest and conflict.

Even with encouragement from Lillian and Burt, who both praised my progress, I was still intimidated by the bureaucratic management I would have to do. Remember, in my days on the streets, I couldn't read, and I always tried to avoid being presented with forms to fill out, menus to read, signs to obey, or anything that exposed my lack of education. Now I had to learn about audio-visual and memorize the standard operating procedures. Then I had to fill out regular forms, create a weekly schedule, issue orders to an audio-visual crew of prisoners, supervise the voting and choosing of television shows, enforce the choices made, and keep inmates from interrupting the TV programs.

I appreciated that the officers trusted me and that so many prisoners asked to be on my crew. I wanted to do well and do my best at my job. But being chief bureaucrat was not my goal. There were so many rules. If someone continued to talk after being warned, he could be written up. That particular "infraction" would result in the loss of half a point (prisoners each started with one hundred points). If a prisoner lost three points, he had to do two hours of community service.

Other infractions in the Honor Dorm life resulted in more community service, and eventually, if you lost too many points, you could be moved out and back into population. Before that happened, the prisoner had to meet with various prison officials and Honor Dorm leaders. The chances for anger, manipulation, and misrepresentation were frequent, but hey, I had a goal of returning to freedom and living a responsible and productive life. My audio-visual leadership seemed to be a step in that direction.

One positive thing was that the other two "community managers" and I could work with prison officials in creating incentives for prisoners to behave well and improve their lives. For example, one of the incentives we asked for was "family night." In other words, if an inmate's points were high enough, he could have two people on his approved list bring in home-cooked food and have a family dinner. We lobbied hard, and the warden and the officers finally approved of family night.

INSIGHT

by Mitchell Rutledge, written while still on death row, but this describes Mitch's abilities that helped him in the Honor Dorm, Holman Prison
March 4, 1986

> *I never was good at reading*
> *And writing*
> *And spelling*
> *But God made up for that*
> *By giving me insight.*
> *See we isn't always able to see*
> *What we are running away from*
> *Because we are too afraid to look back*
> *At what it is.*
> *But the other person see it.*

DREAM

by Mitchell Rutledge
Holman Prison
November 15, 1995

I had a dream last week.
It was about God.
I was praying in my dream in a room
While laying on my back.
I can't say just what the prayer was.
As I prayed all the windows opened up
And wind
And light
Came through the window.
At that time I jumped on the side of the bed
Away from the window.
At that time a voice speak and said
    something.
I can't recall just what it was.
Once I heard the voice I went lower.
Right after the voice
A bolt of lightning hit right beside my head!
I heard the voice right after the lightning.
At that point I woke up!
Cold chills were all over me.
I was so afraid!
Yes, I am very afraid of God.

42

PRISON REFORMS

The one and only positive accomplishment of the prison system is that it keeps dangerous people locked up and away from society. There definitely are people in prisons who are criminally insane—that term is what I would call it, and they should be kept away from society. But many prisoners are capable of living out in society if they change their ways.

Rehabilitation is supposedly a goal of the prison system, but very few prisoners are rehabilitated. They call prison a "correctional institution," but few prisoners are ever corrected and changed. In other words, the prison system itself does not improve inmates. The inmates must rehabilitate themselves. They have to want to change and then move positively to do so. In my case, I became rehabilitated when

I turned to God and firmly decided I would do all I could to change.

Most prisoners get caught up in the negativity of prison life and adapt to it. When they are ultimately released, they are in worse shape than when they arrived. They are older, uneducated, unskilled, and inexperienced in conducting their lives in the larger outside world. So many come right back to prison; in fact, I've seen many who had *wanted* to return to prison and told me they were glad to be back.

How can we expect different results? The prison environment is survival of the fittest. Power belongs to those who are strong and who can manipulate others. Most who come to prison are from a background similar to mine. They had no real father on the scene, they learned little in school, they gravitated toward gangs, and they made money selling drugs or taking part in other illegal activities.

In prison, they have no opportunity or incentive to change. They can't do meaningful work for profit because unions and other groups prohibit cheap labor. Thus, exploitation is where the action is, and the stronger prisoners dominate the weaker. Few rules govern prison life.

Yes, guards are there, but the guards are understandably taught to be wary; they give little opportunity for prisoners to operate outside their narrow lives. Most guards are mechanical and allow only what they have been taught at the academy. Some guards give prisoners little respect and sometimes treat them as subhuman creatures, not much better than animals.

Prisons are overcrowded, which creates great tension, and budgets for states like Alabama are more restricted than ever. It's expensive to house prisoners, and most tax-payers seem satisfied with "locking them up and throwing away the key." Well, okay, but if you do that, don't pretend that any rehabilitation is taking place. Granted, there are evil and dangerous people here in prison. You shouldn't want them outside, and keeping them in prison is the best solution. But most prisoners who come in here could be somewhat rehabilitated without much added expense. If society is going to preach rehabilitation, then some new ideas need to be put into practice.

Maybe we can develop some principles of rehabilitation from my experience. I had a lot going against me, but I did have two things going for me. First, I became a Christian; and second, I had some friends who cared about me, loved me, visited me, and held me accountable.

There are prison ministries that ought to be encouraged to come to prisons all over the country. When I became a Christian, I began to trust in God to learn to read and to bring friends across my path. He helped me with both. And as a Christian I could put my life in perspective. God forgave me, and I didn't have to carry the burden of guilt any longer. I knew God loved me and that I had His help in prison. If more prisoners were Christians, we could improve the atmosphere of prison life and give people hope, not revenge.

Prisoners who have friends and family who care about

them do better than those who don't. Yet much in the prison bureaucracy prevents inmates from making friends or having friends and family visit them very often. The way the visiting list and phone list have been drawn up, inmates are often isolated from the outside world. Visiting, especially from friends, is very restricted.

Also, no prisoner can take an incoming phone call. We have few phones, and phone calls are expensive to make. For many years, a twenty-minute phone call was almost twenty dollars. Inmates were not supposed to have cell phones, so we didn't have any options. Because of all these issues, we made few phone calls, and most families of prison inmates were hurting for cash, so a phone call was a big expense for them.

Finally, the prison system adopted a policy of cheaper phone calls, which really helped me and other inmates as well. I could call Lillian or Anita and Burt and talk for twenty minutes, and the cost was only a few dollars.

I realize that increasing the number of visits and calls would add some work for the prison staff. But if you want to rehabilitate prisoners and increase their ability to survive when they are released, you have to give them quality contact with outsiders, who are essential to the success of those prisoners who are released. If a bitter and lonely prisoner returns to the outside world and steals and kills again, that result is a huge cost to society—larger than the cost of facilitating more phone calls and visits.

With few outside contacts, the prisoners are tied more

strongly to prison life and prison thinking. I know guys in here who are without any contact with another human outside of prison. Yet there may be people, maybe even groups of people, who would adopt a prisoner, get to know him, and become part of his life. A visit from time to time and a few letters make a huge difference. All humans want someone to love them, to care about them, to want to be with them. With visits come a ray of hope, something to look forward to, and contact with the outside that will increase the chance of success in life after release.

WALKING GRAVEYARD

by Mitchell Rutledge
Holman Prison
February 5, 1996

> The phone list has been cut from 10 to 8
>   names.
> They are trying to "discommunicate" us
> From our family and loved ones.
> Everything we have
> They're trying to take away little by little.
> Yes, everything that means our support out
>   there.
> Our minds, souls, and inner freedom are at risk.
> Things isn't getting any better for anyone in
>   my position

PRISON REFORMS

Not *from the state's point of view.*
Guys that are coming to prison
Are becoming more and more disrespectful
Of everything and everyone.
Old timers, such as myself, can't deal with
    those types of guys.
We are as different as day and night.
This is a walking graveyard.
Yes, the walking dead
Once they see life in you,
Begin to hate and wish bad things on you,
Setting up traps for you.
See, once they had life in them.
Seeing it still in you
Is something they can't stand.
Can you see what I'm up against?

43

CLARENCE THOMAS

The difference that even one caring family member can make can be seen in the life of Clarence Thomas. Clarence Thomas and I were both black children born in desperate poverty in the segregated South. Yet one of us is sitting on the Supreme Court of the United States and the other is in prison. Our different lives are not explained by race, by poverty, or by class—we started from the same place. This issue is complex, but I believe family best explains the difference. Justice Thomas had a key male figure, his grandfather, who cared about him and invested in his life. I did not.

I read Clarence Thomas's book, *My Grandfather's Son*, and I was fascinated by the role a father (or grandfather) can play. Clarence's grandfather injected his ideas and concepts into Clarence. Young Clarence always tried to get his grandfather's stamp of approval without truly understanding that his grandfather was always proud of him, although often disappointed with him because of some of his decisions.

Clarence's grandfather made him the person he became and motivated him to strive as hard as he did in life. To put this in perspective, none of my biological brothers or my sister visits me in prison, and rarely do they accept my phone calls or answer my letters. If that was all I had, I would be hopeless—rejected even by my own family. I do appreciate that my brothers, my sister, and some of my relatives testified for me at my two trials. I don't resent them, because I was not there for them when I was outside, and they have troubles of their own without adding my imprisonment to that.

Thanks to the Lord, I have a new family that writes me regularly, remembers my birthday, and expresses their love for me in so many ways that I would not dare to backslide in prison because I couldn't bear to disappoint them. That's been going on for more than thirty years. When temptation comes to do wrong, take offense, or manipulate for personal gain, I often think about them and adjust my behavior. My friends care about me, and I don't intend to disappoint them.

Lillian moved to southern Alabama in 1996. She didn't have a lot of family in California, and we had become such good friends that she wanted to be close to the prison for regular visits. So she packed up everything and moved to Atmore. That meant she could visit me twice a month, every month, which was a great improvement for me. Lillian became a major part of my life after that. She made a big difference.

Lots of people look at her, with her small stature and her friendly, easygoing smile, and they think she is a pushover. Don't let those things fool you. Lillian is a dynamo when she gets interested in something, and I was blessed on the day that she became interested in my case and in me as a person.

Lillian enjoys my poetry. As time passed, I wrote dozens of poems. Lillian compiled my poetry into books to give to people who became interested in my case. She thought that by reading the poems, some person in authority with the state of Alabama might help me one day get out of prison.

I keep hoping for that day.

44

PRISON INCENTIVES

As I wrote earlier, overcrowding greatly affects the present prison system. Most prisons in the United States are overcrowded, which means prison authorities discourage visits and phone calls. There are so many inmates that the prisons can't handle all the family members and friends who want to visit. The phone lists for prisoners also have been cut down, which limits the inmates' chances to stay connected to friends and family members on the outside.

Holman made some improvements in the way it handled visits by putting the vending machines inside the visiting yard and having ice in paper cups available for visitors. But the biggest improvement was when the prison put air-conditioning in the visiting yard. At the same time, overcrowding was getting worse, and the state was looking for options.

About 2005, the state of Alabama passed a regulation that inmates can only have two non-family members as visitors, one female visitor and one male visitor. For me, that suddenly meant that only Lillian and Burt could visit regularly. Anita, Adam, Pam and her family—none of those friends could visit me anymore without all sorts of red tape to get an approved "special visit" from the warden. That was a blow.

Perhaps we need prison committees to meet with the prison administration regularly to work out these personal issues. The goal should be to create an environment that makes released prisoners likely to fit into society and not to come back. Isolating prisoners from their outside friends doesn't help.

Counseling, drug issues, education, and job training also need to be on the table for discussion and action. Unions and other groups prevent prisoners from making products and selling them on the outside. But if inmates could develop skills, they could pay some of their expenses. They could even to some extent repay the families who had crimes committed against them. Perhaps the prisoner could even keep some of this money to help him when he is released. Those kinds of incentives get prisoners thinking more about how to make it once they are released rather than how to use their skills and wit to dominate others inside the prison.

When prisoners are released, some of them would be good in urban missions that reach out to troubled youths. Who better to steer troubled adolescents toward the right path than someone who took the wrong path and has a story to tell about how that failure led to prison? I would very much like to do that. In fact, I am practicing for that role in speeches that I am allowed to make to groups of young people who visit the prison from schools or other organizations. I get out there and tell them bluntly what it is like here, and that speech may help scare away some of them from continuing their bad behavior.

Some of my fellow prisoners have listened to me speak to young people and have approved of my efforts to steer them straight. Isn't that interesting? Even those people who have committed terrible crimes and who seem unrepentant will tell me I did well to discourage others from following the criminal path. All of us deep down know right from wrong. If we will give a few incentives for right behavior in prison, we will have more rehabilitated prisoners and fewer crimes to ruin more lives, clog the court system, and increase the prison population (and the expenses to the tax-payer that go with that).

ANITA'S FIRSTHAND PERSPECTIVE

Mitch makes a strong argument about the devastating effects of overcrowding in our prison systems. Burt and

I have seen that firsthand. At the same time, we always have to keep in mind that the men we see when we are in the prison have committed very serious crimes. The prison system is preventing many of these prisoners from hurting more people, which is vitally important.

Regardless of the overcrowding, inmates need to know that someone on the outside is interested in them personally. Friends or mentors for each inmate can give the prisoners hope and a sense of personal accountability.

When we began visiting Mitch at Holman in 1983, getting into the visiting yards wasn't a problem. Of course, he was on death row then, and many of the death row inmates had no visitors. When he was moved to the prison's general population in 1989, the visiting situation changed as well.

Suddenly, when we were in the visiting yard, every seat was full. As the years passed and the prison became more crowded, we couldn't be sure that we would have all morning for a visit, even if we arrived before 8:00 a.m. If family members of other inmates were waiting to get in after two hours because of the lack of space, we could be asked to leave in order to make room for other visitors. It made no difference that Burt, Adam, and I had often driven hundreds of miles to see Mitch. The waiting families also might have driven a great distance.

The face-to-face visits are vitally important because the visitors from the outside can get a small taste of what prison is like for the inmates, and the inmates are tremendously encouraged when they receive visitors. Many times I have watched prisoners as they entered the visiting yard. Their faces would light up as they hugged their friends and families.

Likewise, when it was time to go, the goodbyes were very hard. Saying goodbye to Mitch was always sad because he wanted so much to be on the outside. Burt and I would have welcomed the opportunity to show Mitch the good part of the outside world that he had never seen. Other inmates on the visiting yard were often saying goodbye to their children who were growing up without them. Or aging parents would look wistfully at their sons who were prisoners—they never expected this kind of outcome for their loved ones.

The visits are most important because each inmate needs to know that someone cares about them individually. The personal attention encourages them to keep on trying to succeed. Mitch's life shows how essential personal relationships are to each man.

Mitch is blessed with a very good mind and a great ability—he calls it "insight"—to relate to others and sense what is going on between individuals. Not all inmates have these advantages, of course, but prisoners would benefit from having an individual on the outside who is interested in them personally: a friend who would write them letters, remember their birthdays, and send Christmas cards. More Christians should step up to the challenge of serving as a mentor to a prisoner. The rewards could change the life of the inmate as well as the life of the mentor. Burt and I have experienced this firsthand as well.

45

NO REHABILITATION

As I said, almost no rehabilitation occurs in prison. True, prison does offer some positive opportunities for self-improvement. We have some education and job-training programs, for example. Prisoners can advance and refine their skills with classes in these areas. But rehabilitation means a change of heart, a desire to do right instead of wrong, and a yearning to fit into society in a productive way. That comes from within and from a willingness to change.

Why is that so hard? Because almost all people who come to prison have had no real guidance, no training to excel, and no foundation for responsible behavior. God is not in their worldview, and when they get here almost all they encounter pushes them away from rehabilitation. The prison world is their new life, and they must be alert to survive in the dog-eat-dog environment.

Economists call this a zero-sum game: when I win, someone else loses. If someone gets something, it is at the expense of someone else. Most inmates follow the dog pack, and that is near anarchy. The strong flourish at the expense of the weak. Physical force, intimidation, and conquest are admired. Most inmates become skilled at survival, and they become even less able to adapt to the outside world if and when they are released.

For example, as I said earlier, I wasn't in prison long before I saw a variety of knife fights. In Hollywood movies about prison, you sometimes see knife fights, but usually in those movies someone wins fairly quickly. In real prison life, some do get killed, but often most survive. Inmates inflict multiple stab wounds on each other, and both will live. Thus, the feuds that sparked the fight persist. You have to sleep with one eye open, so to speak, because you never know when the next round of the fight will begin. Some inmates wait months before seeking revenge.

Prisoners fight over what seems trivial to someone on the outside—someone got a pack of cookies, someone got soup and someone didn't, someone looked at someone improperly, that sort of thing. Often it is a simple misunderstanding. Prisoners will say it's the principle of the thing, but these principles are often unclear. Inmates don't have the social skills to work through the problem.

Sometimes the motives for fights are astonishing. I saw a stabbing once where the guy with the knife was due to be released soon, but he was so adjusted to prison life that he feared release, so he stabbed a guy to make sure he would not be released. That would amaze someone in the outside world because the prison environment is one with too many guys occupying too little space and with too much noise for almost anyone to think straight.

Even if the prisoners were angels, it would be awkward to live here. Inmates have to develop a "prison personality" to survive, and that particular skill does not translate well in the outside world. Because of all these factors, no rehabilitation takes place, and most prisoners who are released commit another crime and return to prison.

PRISON IS A PLACE

by Mitchell Rutledge
Holman Prison
March 6, 1994

> *That is set up to break your spirits.*
> *You really aren't a person, you are a number.*
> *You can make yourself an individual from*
>   *within,*
> *You can tell yourself that you will not*
>   *become*
> *Part of the prison life*

Because once you tell yourself . . .
It's okay to understand
Why this guy have gave up to the gay side
Or why this guy refuse to take care of himself
    anymore
Or why this guy no longer speak of the free
    world
Or why this guy have built his life around his
    prison store
Or why these guys steal or take from each
    other
Or why it's okay
Only two sinks with hot water for 85 to 90
    guys
Or why it's okay while you are eating
A roach is in your food from time to time
Or the plates and glasses you eat and drink
    from
Aren't really clean.
It's okay to understand
We don't have but two or three showers that
    work for 85 to 90 guys
Or why the water is ice cold in the
    wintertime
And too hot to stand under in the
    summertime
Or you try to get a shower before the water
    become cold

And if you get a cold
You won't get the medical treatment you
    need.
Many guys come to believe
Such living conditions are okay.
I can't or should I say I refuse
To understand any of this.
I only live in this condition
Knowing that it isn't forever.

46

LEADERSHIP IN THE HONOR DORM

The creation of the Honor Dorm was a big event in Holman prison. The prison officials supported it because it reinforced their idea that prison could produce genuine rehabilitation. They could assign tasks to the prisoners, hold them accountable, and then say that prison was building character for some. If prisoners failed, they would be sent back to general population; for those who followed the rules, they might get reduced sentences or some other reward.

The prisoners viewed the Honor Dorm differently— many saw it as a chance to live in a safer environment. If they shifted from general population to the Honor Dorm, then they would have less risk of being molested, robbed, or beaten. They didn't particularly want to work harder or be held accountable. They just wanted to live in a safer place.

The original Honor Dorm, set up in 1999, housed 114 inmates out of more than 600 in general population. I applied to get in because I wanted to develop my skills and grow. But some wondered why I was doing that because I had life without parole. What could I gain? Also, unlike many applicants, I was already safe in general population. My reputation and God's protection kept me from harm. But I wanted to go to the next level, so I applied and was accepted into the two-year trial program that became known as the Honor Dorm.

The administrative staff over the Honor Dorm consisted of the warden, who always had the final say, and the assistant warden, the captain, the head of classification, and the chaplain. They were to appoint three community managers, who would govern the Honor Dorm and be accountable to the administration. The community managers had authority over maintenance, service, and entertainment (especially the TV). Since the community managers were accountable to the administration, the managers could make the prisoners accountable for running the Honor Dorm—from painting and fixing faucets to enforcing curfews and supervising the TV.

The prison administration wanted me to become one of the community managers, but I thought that job would be a problem. Prisoners get angry when they don't get what they want, and I didn't want to make enemies in the Honor Dorm.

The chaplain urged me to be a community manager, or at least to apply to become one. I was very uneasy about this and turned him down. I still thought that I worked best by avoiding conflict and leading by example. When I was doing this well, I would have people come up to me and ask me about a problem, and I could try to help them one-on-one.

For example, I had an angry inmate, Patrick, come up to me and say, "I am going to kill Jerry. He borrowed $600 from me and refuses to pay it back." I understood Patrick's point. He wanted not only the money but the respect. If people know they can take from you, they will do so. That's why people get knifed for stealing a pair of shoes. That point, and the money, was where Patrick was focusing. I had to change his focus to change his heart.

I knew Patrick had parents who were involved in his life and anxiously waiting for him to get out of prison. So that's where I started. I got him to think about his parents and what a murder would do to them. Their emotional pain would be terrible, and they would never see him as a free man again. That got Patrick's attention. Then I made this point: "Patrick, you weren't wise to loan anybody in here the huge sum of $600. That is not wise use of the money your parents wanted you to have. You have to take some responsibility here for a bad choice."

Patrick grumbled a bit and went away for a while. The

next week he came up to me and thanked me for encouraging him to change his attitude and causing him to rethink his problem in a different way. He loved his parents, he told me, and couldn't bear to hurt them like that.

Here is my bigger point: I talked with Patrick one-on-one and gave him my best advice. He took it. But if he hadn't taken it, he would have been mad at Jerry, not me. I did with Patrick what God wanted me to do without risking my safety in prison.

I didn't want to give orders, hold people accountable, and write them up if they failed. That would make me a target for disgruntled inmates without giving me much incentive. I wanted to be a counselor, not a CEO.

The administration was pressuring me to take a role, so I became a coordinator, which is less responsibility than a community manager. Still, the coordinator is in a position to create enemies because his job is to make sure everyone else is doing their jobs. I worked two hours each day during the week, overseeing the service crew, the TV crew, and the information crew. If someone had to fix a pipe, I had to make sure he did that. I had to keep daily records and sign the duty roster in the coordinator box.

When some inmates get power, they lord it over others and stick it to them. I only assumed power reluctantly, and I hesitated to go hard on my fellow inmates. When something was not done right, I preferred to give second chances rather than write them up. Some inmates took advantage of me and slacked off in their work. I had to negotiate with them to do what they were supposed to do, and yes, I had to write some of them up. But I tried to be lenient so that when I ultimately wrote someone up, I told him, "You are writing yourself up for not doing your work."

I had the community managers who held me accountable, so I had to hold the inmates under my supervision accountable or the Honor Dorm system would break down. I didn't want to prove to the skeptics that inmates were incapable of governing themselves.

One part of my job I liked was that I could advise the administration on who should get into the Honor Dorm. I wanted to see more young guys get in, and I also wanted to see inmates get the chance to prove they could leave general population and live in safety and order in the Honor Dorm. Sometimes the administration, and even my fellow inmates, would criticize some troubled inmate who had applied. I often heard, "He won't last a week," and "He's the wrong kind of guy for this program."

I fought that by saying, "We all want society to give us another chance, don't we? Do you want the parole board and the judge to reconsider their judgment of you?" That often shut down the skeptics.

Our warden at that time also believed in giving second chances. He recognized that incentives were crucial in changing behavior and making the Honor Dorm work. He searched for incentives that would spark change in inmates. If prisoners wanted early parole as an incentive, and they did, he wanted to prepare them to succeed outside the prison.

For example, he argued that education was important, and so he would bring college professors into the Honor Dorm to teach a class or give a lecture.

One professor I remember spoke effectively to the inmates; as they learned, she became more excited and more capable in her lectures. Her husband even came and spoke to us. We all looked forward to her classes, and she helped take the Honor Dorm to a higher level.

LIFE CIRCLE

by Mitchell Rutledge
Honor Dorm, Holman Prison

Life is such an adventure
In its own right.
We travel through life
Each and every day trying
To achieve the simple task of life
Staying happy and contented in a world full
    of pain and sadness.
As the years pass, we grow older.
Some grow wiser, some grow foolish,
Others become consumed
With pain and madness.

47

BIRDMAN OF ALCATRAZ

In addition to being coordinator in the Honor Dorm, I had to do my "institutional job" as head librarian. I sometimes wondered what my old teachers would think of me as a head librarian, reading books, handing them out, and then collecting them. Some inmates gave me problems collecting books, but I was always able to persuade them to cooperate. When I would be giving out books and collecting them, some inmates would call me "Birdman of Alcatraz," although I felt more like Brooks Hatlen, played by James Whitmore, in *Shawshank Redemption*. Except that he died, and I intended to live.

During my time as librarian, the prison got a computer and began to put its library records on computer. I knew nothing about computers and had to be trained. The inmate who was training me, a college-educated guy, was startled at our first lesson because I thought the monitor was the computer. "Mitch, you know better than that," he said.

I responded, "How am I supposed to know better when I have never seen a computer before? Show me how to use it."

Well, he proved to be a good teacher, and I learned some computer skills.

STRUGGLING PEACE

by Mitchell Rutledge
Honor Dorm, Holman Prison
August 7, 2006

> As I stare into the lives
> That are buried alive with me
> The struggle to have inner peace
> Is fleeing
> We exist in the graveyard in many ways
> We are consumed with the hope
> One day of walking amongst the living once
>   again
>
> For many the struggling peace is fading away
> They find themselves consumed
> With gloom and hopelessness

BIRDMAN OF ALCATRAZ

This life has claimed another soul!
Oh struggling peace within me
I am weary
Gloom is crouching in front of me

Hopelessness stands erect behind me
Waiting to attack
Then I announce from the grave I reside in
In a voice full of confidence
My hope is in God!

48

BURT'S STORY

During the last thirty years, I have seen Mitch blossom from a friendless and almost illiterate person who was one step away from the electric chair to an articulate leader of men. Our relationship started with regular letters, and I slowly watched his clarity increase and his vocabulary grow. After Mitch got off death row, we began to communicate more by phone conversations, about once every three weeks or so. And I have visited him in prison at least once a year since 1984.

You get to know someone in that amount of time. He calls me his older brother, and I write him and talk with him more than I do my own brother and sister. I know Mitch and he knows me. Our backgrounds are different, but what we have in common as humans—our mutual needs, concerns, and challenges—gives us issues we can discuss for hours when we are together.

Our relationship began in encouragement. Christians become generous and kind as they grow in the fruit of the Spirit to do charity and help those in distress. Jesus told us to visit those in prison, after which He said, "Whatever you did for one of the least of these brothers and sisters of mine, you did for me" (Matt. 25:40). So I shared Christ with Mitch in my first letter, and he responded that he had a relationship with the Lord. After that, I encouraged him in his desire to better himself even though he was on death row. Lillian, Anita, and I praised the improvement we saw in his letters to us. He is a quick learner, he is hungry for information, and he is anxious to use his abilities to make a difference.

When Mitch studied for his GED, I told him he was brighter than most of my college students. I said, "Work to your ability, and you will graduate." What a teacher's dream—Mitch loved school! And after he won his GED, we told him to sign up for college classes. We talked about his schoolwork in many of our conversations. After that, the logical next steps were his move to the Honor Dorm and his emergence as a leader there. Lillian, Anita, and I urged him to make that move.

What is sometimes hard for outsiders to grasp is how much Mitch encourages me. We have a relationship, and I am growing in it just as Mitch is. In *The Blind Side*, there is a powerful scene where Leigh Anne Tuohy, played by Sandra Bullock, is having lunch with her upper-middle-class girlfriends. The awkward subject of Leigh Anne's taking in Michael Oher has just come up, and one of the women says, "To open up your home to him. Honey, you're changing that boy's life." Leigh Anne responds, "No, he's changing mine."[1] And that's how it is with Mitch and me. He's changing mine.

Watching Mitch is a wonderful example of the power of the human spirit to triumph over adversity. I teach US history and enjoy describing how John D. Rockefeller became the first billionaire in US history even though his father was a wandering bigamist. Abraham Lincoln's mother was illiterate and his father barely earned a living, but Lincoln became a powerful writer and a great president. Students need to hear what others have overcome, and Mitch is always on my heart in what he has overcome and how much he is adding to society.

With Mitch in mind, I designed a lecture on Harriet Tubman, the former slave, and Thomas Garrett, a Delaware Quaker who ran the Underground Railroad. I stress how much can be done when black and white work together. Tubman courageously smuggled slaves into Delaware; and Garrett, also at great personal risk, tried to sneak them into freedom in Philadelphia. At one point Garrett was caught and lost all his possessions. Black and white worked hand in hand to support the principles of the Declaration of Independence.

My friendship with Mitch is personal. He is gifted as a counselor, and I need his advice to keep my own relationships strong. With all the problems he faces in prison, I used to feel guilty using up our phone time or our visiting time asking for help with my own lesser problems, but Mitch insists on it. When he tries to get me to see my problem from a different angle, he will often start by saying, "Now, big brother, I understand what you are feeling, but . . ." and then comes the gentle advice.

About fifteen years ago, I was asking him for help with an ongoing discussion I was having with Anita that concerned several decisions about my work and our personal life. Mitch abruptly asked, "Where is your wedding ring?"

I said, "I lost it swimming in the Atlantic Ocean. It was uncomfortable on my finger, and I didn't replace it."

Mitch asked me to look at the issue from another angle. My wedding ring, he said, was a statement to Anita that I was hers only. Not wearing it, especially since I was around so many students, might be a negative signal to Anita. Immediately after that prison visit, I bought another wedding ring. Anita liked that, and it was a step in the right direction for me. I'm still wearing it fifteen years later.

My relationship with Mitch is not one-sided. Ron Myers, the prosecuting attorney, could not conceive of Mitch actually adding value to my life, and our friction at the two sentencing trials reflected Myers's misperception. He would bait me by asking sarcastically how Mitch could possibly impart wisdom to a college professor. Myers must have believed *Time* magazine when it said Mitch was "defective" and we should "forget him."[2] He couldn't see that Mitch is a valuable friend because he is very smart about human relationships, and human nature is constant across economic, class, and educational lines.

Mitch's insights into human nature have helped him work out a system for success in prison life. I have enjoyed watching this story play out during my prison visits. In the 1980s, when I would visit, Mitch was still concerned that Anita and I might desert him. He was on death row and knew few prisoners. In the visiting room he tended to be aloof from them and focused on Anita and me. In the 1990s, finally off death row, Mitch began mingling with the general prison population. In the visiting room he would tell us about the other prisoners in the room. He knew them well.

In the 2000s, Mitch was a leader in the Honor Dorm, and I was both proud and amused to watch him work the visiting room. Sometimes prisoners would come up to Mitch and ask him for advice right there during my visit. Also, Mitch would take time to walk around and speak with every prisoner in the room. I told him he was like an old-time Tammany Hall ward heeler working his constituents. They all showed him respect.

But Mitch at heart is not a politician or just a guy trying to survive and get along. He wants to make a difference. He is propelled by his desire to make his life meaningful, and without friends, life has much less meaning to Mitch. Lillian, Anita, Pam, Rachel, Bill, Gwen, and I are his small group of outside friends, and we mean something to him. If one of us is threatened, Mitch is upset. When one of the inmates said a slur directed at Lillian, Mitch abandoned his prison survival mode and slapped the inmate—ready to take the challenge from the knives held by the inmate and his friends.

In *The Blind Side*, Leigh Ann discovers that Michael scored at the 98 percent level in "protective instincts,"[3] and that is where Mitch would score as well. If a prisoner had attacked Anita or me in prison, Mitch would have defended us with his life. His prison survival mode is his way of negotiating a tough prison situation.

Lillian and I have visited Mitch together five times in the last year, and we continue to enjoy Mitch's sense of humor. (Anita and Adam can't visit Mitch now because of prison reductions in the number of guests on the visitor lists.) On one of these visits, Mitch and Lillian got into a heated argument—like a brother and sister—about a call Lillian wanted to make to a prison official. Mitch thought the call would be unwise, and I gingerly supported him. But Lillian prevailed. When she left the table to buy a drink from the vending machine, Mitch, with a twinkle in his eye, turned to me and said, "We're getting better. The two of us together almost talked her out of it."

49

I DO A VIDEO

One day when I was typing on the computer, the warden came in looking for me. I greeted him and noticed a camera crew with him, and that really got my curiosity going. I recognized the local district attorney, who had helped start me as a speaker with tour groups of troubled kids. I did that for a while, but the program had been stopped.

Eight years earlier we had connected when he heard about my interest in keeping prisons safe and keeping at-risk kids out of prison. He came to prison, called on me for a visit, and challenged me with three questions: "What would you tell your sixteen-year-old daughter who you discover is now pregnant? What would you tell your sixteen-year-old son who is talking about committing suicide? What would you tell a sixteen-year-old boy you met who is wanting to commit suicide?"

I pondered those questions and started to say something, but the DA stopped me. "No," he said. "Write me a page on each one of them. Send it to the warden, and he will get it to me."

I went back to my cell block and thought about my answers. I talked with some of the inmates and many were negative. "Why play their game?" they said. "Besides, you have life without parole. This won't help you. Why do it?"

But I disagreed. I had a chance to make a difference, so I wrote answers to those three questions and sent them to the warden.

Two weeks later, the DA was back with cameras. "I liked your answers," he said. "How would you like to put them on video?"

"What do you mean by that?" I asked.

He replied, "We want to make a tape to help the young kids who have not reached a high level of crime. And hearing from guys like you can only help them."

I said yes, and he asked if I knew other guys who might also give testimony. I thought of a few, and the warden came up with one or two as well.

Some of the guys I asked didn't want to do it, but we ended up with four or five others who joined me in creating the video "Make the Right Choice." I wanted this video to work and did my best to persuade viewers to go straight. In my presentation, I held out both of my hands and said,

"Each day we have to make choices." I then spelled out the consequences of making the right choices—school, job, family, and career—and also the wrong choices—rebelling against authority, crime, jail, and prison, which I described in frightening detail.

I wanted students to see both of my outstretched hands and see that the choice was theirs. They controlled their futures by the choices they made. I wanted the kids to think long term—to get a vision for their life and its possibilities. The other inmates on the video also said good things—I was proud of the job we did—and our video was shown in many schools in the county.

I did my best in that video, but afterward I didn't think much about it. I knew the message was getting out because when I was on the visiting yard, sometimes kids would recognize me and call out to me. They remembered my outstretched arms and the choices I was presenting to them.

So after eight years, I was glad to see the DA again, and he welcomed me like an old friend. "Hi Mitch, it's been a long time," he said. He introduced me to his friends in suits and ties. He had high praise for our "Make the Right Choice" video. "Mitch," he said, "that video is now part of the Alabama school curriculum and has also been accepted in two other states. One county that is showing the tape is claiming that their truancy rate has sharply declined." I looked pleased, and he said, "I just want you to know the difference you are making in lives. And the other guys did too. Nice job, all of you."

Our warden was new, and all this positive publicity pleased him very much. At least that is what I learned later. He called me into his office and I didn't know what he wanted—often such calls are bad news—so I was nervous. But when I came in, he said, "I liked your tape."

I smiled.

"You and the others did a good job. I also see that you at one time would speak to the tours coming through this camp."

"Yes," I replied, "until it was stopped."

"Well, would you like to start back?" he asked.

"Sure," I said.

And true to his word, shortly thereafter, the officer in my cell block called me and said the warden needed me to speak to a tour. I shaved and got a clean set of clothes and got ready to speak again to a tour. Before they came in, I saw their uniforms and could see they were at-risk kids. That's my favorite kind because that is where I might really be able to make a difference.

Once I was doing speeches again, the pressure increased for me to become one of the three community managers. The Honor Dorm was changed into the Faith Dorm, and those who went through the two years and did their jobs without being kicked out were called the "permanent party." They would be taking the leadership roles in the new Faith Dorm. This time the selection of community managers would be different. The administration, instead of appointing community managers, now supported elections. And I had many inmates urging me to run.

"Mitch," several of them said, "we need you up there to fight for what we want, not what they want us to do."

I reluctantly agreed to run. I received the top vote total and became a community manager with greater responsibility and regular meetings with the warden, the assistant warden, the head of classification, and the chaplain.

MY SOUL

by Mitchell Rutledge
Honor Dorm, Holman Prison

A friend asked me about my Soul.
The question was, do you know where your
Soul is?
In which direction is it heading?
I was weak in response.
I wanted to understand her meaning behind
the question.
I wanted to give her the best answer that was
in me.
This required some thinking.
Here is what I came up with.

My Soul is heading in the direction
Of the Truth and the Light.
However it isn't an easy journey.
There are all types of stumbling blocks to
hurdle.

I never once stop reaching for God.
With this I live, understanding that God
   know my struggles.
With Faith in God
My Soul is on a never-ending path to God
And so I live!
That's where my Soul is!

50

SPEAKING TO AT-RISK YOUTHS

As a new community manager, I was busy with meet-ings, paperwork, and enforcing rules. Also, I spoke to tour groups on Wednesdays, I attended a required class, and I still had duties as librarian. All this was not easy for me, but it improved me and made me more capable. No, it wasn't easy to fire an entire maintenance crew of ten people or even to supervise the TV.

TV in the evenings is a special time for inmates but also a source of contention. I had to supervise votes on what shows to watch, and I had to enforce no-talking rules. Even the voting was tricky because some inmates would urge friends, who didn't care to watch, to come in and vote for their show. So we developed a rule that everyone who voted had to stay to watch at least half the show. That way we at least had serious voters, even if some were outraged when they lost the vote.

Incentives were the keys to the success of the Faith Dorm. Why should someone leave general population to fulfill the requirements of the Faith Dorm unless he had some incentive? True, the Faith Dorm was safer, but we needed to be more than just a reprieve from violence. The warden wanted to build character, and we tried to help him come up with incentives that would work for everyone. Early parole was a start, but what about those of us with life without parole? I talked with many inmates, and we fought for more incentives for the men in the Faith Dorm, for privileges that would allow them to eat better or share more time with family members.

In turn, the warden wanted those in the Faith Dorm to do the work of running the dorm and also to improve themselves by taking special classes. The warden was leaning on me, and other leaders in the Faith Dorm, to be accountable and enforce the rules. He wanted no drug problems and lots of self-improvement. But I was also getting pressure from inmates to increase incentives. Some inmates resented me and wanted the power I so reluctantly held. I told the chaplain I would do this job for a year and then I wanted out. But during that year I had the chance to help make the Faith Dorm work better.

We got better people in key leadership positions, and that improved morale. We also overturned some bad policies. As an example, we had a 10:30 night curfew, when lights had to be out and we had to be reasonably quiet. Some of those in power wanted to write people up for minor violations. I thought that was silly, and I also thought curfew should expand to 2:00 in the morning on weekends. We had a game room, and lots of guys liked to play dominos and hang out there at night. Why not let them do that on weekends? We won that concession and that made the Faith Dorm even better. It improved our morale and made us more cohesive as a group.

After one year as a community manager, I told the chaplain, "I am ready to pass the torch." After two months, there was no action, so I reminded him of my pledge to do my best to make the Faith Dorm work well, but that one year and two months was enough. One month later he appointed my replacement, and I scaled back to my duties as librarian and a speaker to tour groups. But another opportunity was on the way.

I was going to get the chance to be a teacher. Lillian and Burt are both teachers, and I've enjoyed hearing them talk over the years about their jobs. Also, I believe teaching is a way to make a difference—without annoying as many people as you do when you are community manager.

A PRAYER FOR HELP AND UNDERSTANDING

by Mitchell Rutledge
Honor Dorm, Holman Prison

Dear God,

Please do not let me drown in Despair.
God, allow peace and joy to ring within my
heart.
God, lead my feet away from the path of
Despair
Because if not, I don't feel I can do it on my
own.
God, my Vision is only for the present,
The things at hand are all I know.
However, God, your Vision is timeless.
Fear have took over me,
I am afraid of what the next moment may
bring
Because of my fear of being conquered by
Despair.
God, you understand what I am going
through.
You know my heart, so please come to my
rescue.
Save me, I am feeling so alone and afraid in
this world.
Let tomorrow be the day of understanding
myself,
My relationship with you.
And God, please bring and continue to keep
love

And understanding between me and my
*   friends,*
Especially my soul mate.
Thank you, God.

51

TEACHER

The teaching opportunity started when one of the reg-ular teachers, the guy who taught me about computers, wanted to increase his administrative role as chaplain's assistant. He would have to give up teaching a class, and he wanted me to replace him. I was anxious to get the chance to teach, but the guy over the GED program in the Faith Dorm told the chaplain he didn't think I was ready for that responsibility.

The warden knew me, and he overruled the GED teacher. My class would be the introductory class for the new guys in the Faith Dorm. It was on "life skills." I would be teaching once a week for twenty-six weeks on how to live effectively in prison, so that after being released, inmates could succeed outside of prison. Then, after twenty-six weeks of my introduction to life skills, the new guys would go to a second-semester class.

I was nervous about facing my peers. I knew firsthand how disrespectful they can be to teachers. If the prisoners are bored, or if they disagree with the teacher, then they will show their contempt very clearly. Sure, my speaking to tours had been good practice, but facing wide-eyed teenagers was different from facing hardened criminals. The curriculum I was to teach had some good material and structure and it centered on coping skills, which all inmates need in prison. When the administration gave me the class guides for the twenty-six classes, I looked at them and said a prayer. I would need God's guidance to succeed at my new job.

At 9:00 a.m. on a Wednesday, I began my first forty-five-minute class. I was self-conscious as I studied the faces of the thirty prisoners in front of me. I spoke clearly and used examples and stories to connect with them, and their faces softened a bit. I began to really like what I was doing. Thirty minutes after my class, I spoke to a tour group; giving back-to-back speeches became a pattern for the next twenty-six weeks.

I was getting a lot of practice in public speaking, and I could often see the effect of my words on my audiences. That encouragement made me bolder, and I steadily improved. The counselors for the at-risk youths began bringing in more and more groups for me to address, and even a few of the guards and the nurses in the prison began asking me to speak to their children.

Earlier I had thought that resigning as community manager would free up my time, but now I was working harder than ever—but enjoying it more because I would rather speak to a crowd than enforce discipline on them. Sometimes a counselor or student would ask me when I was getting out of prison.

"I have life without parole," I would say, and they often responded, "That is sad. We need you out here."

I would smile and agree, "Yes, I need to be out there."

I may still have been in prison, but my self-worth was growing.

Each week I would get in front of the inmates and teach them how to communicate, how to conduct themselves with integrity, and how to be effective and survive in prison. I was connecting with them—I could tell by the questions they asked. Then came something unexpected: the class started growing because members of the permanent party—those who had passed the class and had lived in the Faith Dorm for two years—started coming to my class instead of the ones they were taking. We didn't have room to fit them all in, and it created an imbalance because other classes were shrinking in size.

The administration announced that no more inmates from the permanent party could attend my class. Then the chaplain called in some of the members of the permanent party and asked them why they wanted to go to my class. I found out later that they responded, "Because Mitch speaks our language. He knows what we need to hear."

In my next class, the uproar about class attendance was bubbling over, and so I began the class by saying, "They say I speak your language. Yes, I'm on you guys' level, and the other classes must be on a higher level than we are."

Actually that remark got me in trouble. Some people were resenting my success, and the administration was puzzled over how to react to what was happening. I had to go before the community managers on the charge that I had violated standard operating procedure by undermining teaching authority in the classes. I never received any punishment for "undermining SOP," and my class continued to grow in spite of the new rule limiting its size.

I also continued to speak to at-risk kids and to do my library duties. I always preached peace, and I became known—especially among the tour groups—as the guy with the outstretched arms. On one hand, I gave the consequences of bad choices, and on the other hand, I would describe the consequences and the future for those who made wise choices. That was my message then and still is now. From the time you wake up in the morning till the time you go to bed, you will make choices, and those choices will have consequences. According to the sociologists, I'm the guy who makes the case for deferred gratification.

Some inmates liked what I was doing, and others opposed me. We should expect those results when we step out in faith. I'm accountable to God, not to man, for my actions, and different men were affected in different ways by what I was doing.

52

I SAVE A LIFE

One night, in the midst of turmoil, I had the most humbling experience of my life. I was playing checkers with an inmate, trying to find some peace in the middle of the prison noise, when an inmate rushed toward me gasping for breath.

"Mitch, I just saw you on TV. You are on the news."

"What?" I said in disbelief. "Don't play mind games with me."

"Really," he insisted, but I let it go.

Then he called another guy over and asked, "Who did you just see on the news?"

The guy responded, "Mitch."

Others were agreeing with them, so I went over to the

TV room to investigate. The guys said the network had just finished a news story on the "Make the Right Choice" video that was being shown in the schools.

Since the six o'clock local news is usually repeated at nine o'clock, I decided to come in at nine and see what was said. Sure enough, there was the story on our "Make the Right Choice" video and the impact it was having. The reporter was interviewing a young guy and his mother, and the young guy held out both of his hands and said that the guy on the tape did that and said on one hand is one set of choices that leads to prison and on the other hand is a set of choices that leads to freedom, career, wife, and family.

The kid said he decided to change his life. "He saved my life," he said. His mom was standing there smiling, and she thanked me over the air for stopping her son from continuing to make bad decisions and for saving her son's life.

I was so touched, so moved, by what I saw that I could barely leave the room and get over to my bed. I just lay down and reflected. On one hand, I had taken a life, and the consequences of that decision were permanent. But on the other hand, a young man was saying I saved his life. And the consequences of that may be etched on the pages of history someday.

53

FINAL CHAPTER
WHAT I HAVE LEARNED

When I think back on my life, I know that God is real and that He intervened in my life to turn things around. I had to ask Him to do that, because the Lord doesn't force Himself on anybody. I had to learn to live His way. But when I think about the way I learned to read, the way He gave me a "family" outside of prison, the way He has protected me all these years in prison—I know that the Lord is part of my life.

I hope my story will lead others to ask Jesus to come into their hearts and change them. The Lord changed me when I was a mess as a human being, and He can change anyone who asks Him into their heart. As it says in Romans 10:13, "Everyone who calls on the name of the Lord will be saved."

EPILOGUE
BURT AND ANITA FOLSOM

As we write these words, Mitch is still in prison. He was transferred recently from Holman to another maximum-security prison outside Birmingham. He has been incarcerated in jails and prisons since January 1981.

During these many years, Mitch has experienced the faithfulness of God and how true He is to His Word. That faith has rehabilitated Mitch more than anything else.

Mitch has maintained his friendships with the people he has come to know outside of prison by writing thousands of letters over the years. All of us, including Lillian, Pam and her sisters and brother, call ourselves Mitch Rutledge's family, and we feel privileged to have witnessed his remarkable growth into a man who is self-controlled, self-educated, and eager to give back to society. Mitch puts more into his friends than he takes out.

Yes, he has worked to overcome the problems of his younger years, and the prison staff has given him opportunities in the Honor Dorm and in speaking to youth groups. He has a record of good behavior throughout his time in prison. There may be no inmate in the United States who is more rehabilitated than Mitchell Rutledge. Surely he has paid his debt to society and should be given special consideration for parole.

Burton and Anita Folsom
Hillsdale, Michigan / Atlanta, Georgia
March 31, 2015

NOTES

CHAPTER 1: THIS IS MY STORY

1. Kurt Andersen, "An Eye for an Eye," *Time* magazine, January 24, 1983, http://content.time.com/time/magazine/article/0,9171,950821,00.html.

CHAPTER 3: COLUMBUS, GEORGIA

1. Population of the 100 Largest Urban Places, US Bureau of the Census, June 15, 1998, https://www.census.gov/population/www/documentation/twps0027/tab20.txt.

19: NEW FRIENDS—AT LAST!

1. Andersen, "An Eye for an Eye."

CHAPTER 35: GED

1. Booker T. Washington, *Up From Slavery* (New York: Doubleday, Page & Co., 1908), 27.
2. Ibid.

CHAPTER 48: BURT'S STORY

1. *The Blind Side*, directed by John Lee Hancock (Burbank, CA: Warner Home Video, 2010), DVD.
2. Andersen, "An Eye for an Eye."
3. Hancock, *The Blind Side*.

ABOUT THE AUTHORS

Anita Folsom has directed Hillsdale College's Free Market Forum since 2006. She has written for the *Wall Street Journal*, the *Detroit News*, *Continuity*, the *American Spectator*, *Human Events*, and other publications. She is the coauthor, with her husband, Burt, of *FDR Goes to War* (Simon & Schuster, 2011) and *Uncle Sam Can't Count* (HarperCollins, 2014). Before becoming a writer, she worked in politics and served in the Electoral College in 1988. Anita has appeared on numerous television programs and given many radio interviews. Anita and her husband write for their blog at BurtFolsom.com.

Burt Folsom currently holds the Charles Kline Chair in History and Management at Hillsdale College. He has written for dozens of publications, including the *Wall Street Journal*, *Business History Review*, and the *Washington Times*. Burt has written eight books, including the best-sellers *Myth of the Robber Barons* and *New Deal or Raw Deal*. He has made numerous television appearances and is a frequent guest on talk radio. Burt and his wife, Anita, write for their blog at BurtFolsom.com.